managing
YOURSELF

T0349209

managing
YOURSELF

BERNICE WALMSLEY

PART OF HACHETTE LIVRE UK

Orders: Please contact Bookpoint Ltd, 130 Milton Park, Abingdon, Oxon OX14 4SB. Telephone: (44) 01235 827720, Fax: (44) 01235 400454. Lines are open from 9.00 to 5.00, Monday to Saturday, with a 24-hour message answering service. You can also order through our website www.hoddereducation.co.uk.

British Library Cataloguing in Publication Data
A catalogue record for this title is available from the British Library.

ISBN-13: 978 0340 947388

First published   2010
Impression number   10 9 8 7 6 5 4 3 2 1
Year   2013 2012 2011 2010

Typeset by Transet Limited, Coventry, England.
Printed in Great Britain for Hodder Education, an Hachette Livre UK Company, 338 Euston Road, London NW1 3BH, by Cox & Wyman, Reading, Berkshire RG1 8EX.

Hachette Livre UK's policy is to use papers that are natural, renewable and recyclable products and made from wood grown in sustainable forests. The logging and manufacturing processes are expected to conform to the environmental regulations of the country of origin.

The Chartered Management Institute

CMI

The Chartered Management Institute is the only chartered professional body that is dedicated to management and leadership. We are committed to raising the performance of business by championing management.

We represent 86,000 individual managers and have 450 corporate members. Within the Institute there are also a number of distinct specialisms, including the Institute of Business Consulting and Women in Management Network.

We exist to help managers tackle the management challenges they face on a daily basis by raising the standard of management in the UK. We are here to help individuals become better managers and companies develop better managers.

We do this through a wide range of products and services, from practical management checklists to tailored training and qualifications. We produce research on the latest 'hot' management issues, provide a vast array of useful information through our online management information centre, as well as offering consultancy services and career information.

You can access these resources 'off the shelf' or we can provide solutions just for you. Our range of products and services is designed to ensure organisations and managers develop their potential and excel. Whether you are at the start of your career or a proven performer in the boardroom, we have something for you.

We engage policy makers and opinion formers and, as the leading authority on management, we are regularly consulted on a range of management issues. Through our in-depth research and regular policy surveys of members, we have a deep understanding of the latest management trends.

For more information visit our website **www.managers.org.uk** or call us on **01536 207307**.

Chartered Manager

Transform the way you work

The Chartered Management Institute's Chartered Manager award is the ultimate accolade for practising professional managers. Designed to transform the way you think about your work and how you add value to your organisation, it is based on demonstrating measurable impact.

This unique award proves your ability to make a real difference in the workplace.

Chartered Manager focuses on the six vital business skills of:

- Leading people
- Managing change
- Meeting customer needs
- Managing information and knowledge
- Managing activities and resources
- Managing yourself

Transform your organisation

There is a clear and well-established link between good management and improved organisational performance. Recognising this, the Chartered Manager scheme requires individuals to demonstrate how they are applying their leadership and change management skills to make significant impact within their organisation.

Transform your career

Whatever career stage a manager is at Chartered Manager will set them apart. Chartered Manager has proven to be a stimulus to career progression, either via recognition by their current employer or through the motivation to move on to more challenging roles with new employers.

But don't take just our word for it ...

Chartered Manager has transformed the careers and organisations of managers in all sectors.

- *'Being a Chartered Manager was one of the main contributing factors which led to my recent promotion.'*
  Lloyd Ross, Programme Delivery Manager, British Nuclear Fuels

- *'I am quite sure that a part of the reason for my success in achieving my appointment was due to my Chartered Manager award which provided excellent, independent evidence that I was a high quality manager.'*
  Donaree Marshall, Head of Programme Management Office, Water Service, Belfast

- *'The whole process has been very positive, giving me confidence in my strengths as a manager but also helping me to identify the areas of my skills that I want to develop. I am delighted and proud to have the accolade of Chartered Manager.'*
  Allen Hudson, School Support Services Manager, Dudley Metropolitan County Council

- *'As we are in a time of profound change, I believe that I have, as a result of my change management skills, been able to provide leadership to my staff. Indeed, I took over three teams and carefully built an integrated team, which is beginning to perform really well. I believe that the process I went through to gain Chartered Manager status assisted me in achieving this and consequently was of considerable benefit to my organisation.'*
  George Smart, SPO and D/Head of Resettlement, HM Prison Swaleside

To find out more or to request further information please visit our website **www.managers.org.uk/cmgr** or call us on **01536 207429**.

Contents

CHAPTER 03

CHAPTER 04

CHAPTER 05

CHAPTER 06

CHAPTER 07

CHAPTER 08

CHAPTER 09

CHAPTER 10

CHAPTER 11

CHAPTER 12

Foreword

There has never been a greater need for better management and leadership skills in the UK. As we've seen over the past couple of years, it's all too often the case that management incompetence takes the blame for high-profile, costly and sometimes tragic failures. Put this in the context of a world dominated by changing technology and growing international competition, and every manager in this country has a responsibility for ensuring that he or she has the best possible skills to contribute to successful business performance.

So it is alarming that just one in five managers in the UK are professionally qualified. The truth is that we spend less on management development in the UK than our European competitors. Effectively this means that, if you want to develop professionally, if you want to boost your career chances, or if you just want recognition for the work you do, the onus is on you – the individual – to improve your skills. What it also means is that all of us – individual managers, employers and policy makers – need to answer difficult questions about how well equipped we are to lead in the 21st century. Are our standards slipping? How capable are we when it comes to meeting the skill requirements of modern business? Studies show that project management, alliance-building and communication skills are the three key 'over-arching' skills that must be mastered by the successful manager. But how many people can honestly claim they have mastery over all three?

In recent years the news has been dominated by stories focusing on breathtaking management failures. The collapse of the banking sector has been much-analysed and will continue to be discussed in the years to come. It's not just the private sector. Vast amounts of column inches have been devoted to investigations of failures across the health and social care sector, too. The spotlight has also been on management, at an individual level, as the recession deepened in the aftermath of the banking crisis, with dramatic rises in the UK's unemployment levels. Many managers are fighting an ongoing battle to control costs and survive with reduced credit and slowing demand. They are also struggling to prove their worth, to show they meet required standards now, and in the long-term.

But imagine a world where management and leadership enables top-class performance right across British businesses, the public sector and our not-for-profit organisations – where management isn't a byword for bureaucracy and failure, but plays a real role in boosting performance. The way to achieve such a realistic utopia is by developing the skills that will help you, as a manager, perform to the best of your capability. And that is why this book will help. Its aim is to provide you with practical, digestible advice that you can take straight from the pages to apply in your working environment.

Does any of this matter? Well, you wouldn't want your accounts signed off by someone lacking a financial qualification. You certainly wouldn't let an unqualified surgeon anywhere near you with a scalpel, nor would you seek an unqualified lawyer to represent your interests. Why, then, should your employer settle for management capability that is second best? It means that you need to take time out to develop your skills so that these can be evaluated and so you can stand out from the competition.

What's more, managers will play a critical role in determining how well the UK meets a wide range of challenges over the next decade. How can managers foster innovation to promote economic growth? How do they tackle the gender pay gap and the continued under-representation of women in the boardroom, as part of building truly fair, diverse organisations? Managers in all sectors will need to learn how to lead their teams through the changes we face; they will also need to be able to manage change. Above all, managers will need to grasp the nettle when it comes to managing information and knowledge. The key will rest in how they learn to manage themselves.

First-class management and leadership really can drive up both personal and corporate performance. It can boost national productivity and enhance social wellbeing. If you want to be the best manager you can be, this book is for you. In one go it will provide you with practical advice and the experience of business leaders. It is also a fascinating and enthralling read!

Ruth Spellman OBE
Chief Executive
Chartered Management Institute

01

Introduction

Who should read this book?

If you want to upgrade your management skills, then this series of books – a sub-strand of the Instant Manager series – is for you. The series covers a range of skills needed by today's managers including those set out in the employer-led set of standards (the National Occupational Standards) for leadership and management drawn up to improve the productivity and profitability of organisations in the UK. These standards are also aimed at helping with career development so are of benefit to employees and employers alike.

This book is for any manager – new or experienced – who needs help with managing their own skills, time and development in their working life. It is not jargon-filled or too complicated and theory-bound. It contains practical advice to help you in your working life. So, if you need to acquire the knowledge needed to make sure that you have the personal resources vital for you to do your job effectively then this book will help you to acquire the necessary skills. It will also help you to achieve that elusive work/life balance by taking a holistic view.

A range of topics, linked by the common themes of understanding and enhancing your own skills set in relation to your work role, is covered in each book in the form of ten questions on the topic plus an interview with a well-known business expert. In this book you will find the answers to questions that will show you how to manage yourself. First, you will assess your own current resources and learn how to fill any gaps in your knowledge and skills, establishing a plan for your personal development. You will then learn about how your personal networks can help you in your work role and how you can develop them to your advantage now and in the future.

At the end of each chapter, after a specific question has been answered, there will be a summary of the chapter and a short action checklist, which will give you a series of practical steps that you will need to take to overcome the challenge of that aspect of managing yourself.

The skills that you will learn in this book are vital to your success as a manager; you will also obtain tips on how to balance your work and the rest of your life to make the most of what you have. Of course, the skills you need are many and varied, so in this book we will be concentrating on the ones you need to manage your personal resources – your knowledge, skills and competencies, to ensure your professional development and to develop your personal networks

What skills do you need to manage yourself?

Many of the skills necessary to manage yourself are those that all managers will need – the general skills that you will use every day. But all managers need to manage their own personal resources (including the skills, knowledge and competencies they have acquired), and there are specific skills that will be vital if you are to ensure that you have all the personal resources you need to fulfil your work role successfully – now and in the future.

General management skills such as communication and objective setting will be vital when you are identifying and agreeing your work role and more specific ones such as time management will be vital in using your time effectively, especially when undertaking new activities that you may identify as necessary. Finally, self-assessment and reviewing skills will be necessary when identifying any gaps in your current skills.

Let's look in a little more detail at the skills that will be necessary to manage yourself successfully:

- **Self-assessment** – the most obvious aspect of managing yourself is knowing yourself. You will need to conduct a thorough and honest assessment of your skills, knowledge, understanding and time, and then use it to improve your performance. This is dealt with extensively in the first few chapters.
- **Setting objectives** – when trying to improve anything it is vital to take an organised approach and a first step in this is to set objectives so that you have something to aim at that will produce the required improvements. The chapter on objectives will show you how objectives can help and how to set SMART objectives – i.e. objectives that are Specific, Measurable, Achievable, Realistic and Time-bound.
- **Obtaining feedback** – objective feedback is useful in showing you where your performance can be improved (and, hopefully, where it is good enough not to need improvement) and if used effectively will allow you to set up a personal development plan that will lead to your future progress.

- **Personal networking** – while we all have personal networks including friends, neighbours, family and work colleagues, you may not have considered how they can be developed so that they help you in your career. The two chapters on personal networking will show you how networks can help you in your work role and how you can develop effective, wide-ranging personal networks so that you can exchange information and resources.

What will lead to career success?

Although some people seem to just arrive in a job that is perfect for them without much evidence of great effort or planning, this is very rarely the case. Even today, in the celebrity culture that has developed involving 'instant' stardom after a brief appearance on a reality show, it is highly unlikely that little or no effort has gone in to that success. If you delve into any successful person's background you will find that they have been working long and hard for that 'overnight' success. That celebrity who seems to have appeared out of nowhere will have been attending singing and drama classes and turning up for auditions, spending all their time on their life's dream. Similarly, any top business person will have been working hard on career development and on building up a business as well as working on their own skills to prepare themselves and to achieve their goals. So, for your career to develop and to be successful you will have to put in the effort. To succeed in any field you will need:

- determination
- an organised approach

- an understanding of what you need to learn
- a vision of where you want to be.

In the forthcoming chapters you will go through a process of self-assessment to see how you can manage yourself to best effect in terms of career management, job success, personal development and achieving a work/life balance.

Let's now move on to the challenges that will meet you in answering the first of our questions, which looks at the personal resources you need to carry out your work role.

02

What personal resources do you need to do your job?

It is important to know what skills, aptitudes and attitudes that you need to possess in order to be able to do your job. You must make sure that you also possess the specific knowledge that the work role requires and that you have the time to carry out your duties properly. This knowledge of yourself will help you to see not only what you can do but also what you cannot do. So, your first task in managing yourself is to see just what you have to offer. Who are you? How do you perform? What is important to you? To answer these questions and then to see which of your personal resources you are using in your current work role you should consider a wide variety of areas about yourself.

Skills

Skills are those things that we have learned to do such as swimming, using a software program or understanding the intricacies and implications of a balance sheet. With a bit of thought it should be a relatively easy task to make a list of all the skills you have learned. Start with those that you use on a day-to-day basis in your work and then develop your list further by adding all the things you have learned in your personal life such as creative crafts, driving a car or speed reading. Lots of the things that you may think of as unrelated to work will have some relevance to your working life. Driving, for example, may not be a skill valued by your current employer if you are at a desk all day but in the future this may be an essential skill if you have to visit customers.

Abilities

Abilities are different from skills in that they are things that come naturally to us rather than having to be learned. This may include things such as persuasive capabilities, dancing and getting organised (although, of course you can learn to improve and expand many of your abilities).

Values

Values are the things that are important to you. They could encompass widely varying aspects such as patriotism and punctuality. Being aware of your values is an important part of knowing yourself and it is only when you know yourself that you can plan your personal and career development effectively. Values are also important in that it is highly desirable to work in an organisation that has values that are not at odds with your own. There is more about values in Chapter 9.

Attitudes

When you list your attitudes you will find that some are highly desirable such as being enthusiastic, tolerant or compassionate, while others may be less so – such as impatience or intolerance. However, most attitudes have positive and negative aspects. For example, tolerance can, in some circumstances be viewed as someone being too easy going, so try to see all aspects of the attitudes you have and how they might affect your working life now and in the future.

Knowledge

Everyone, no matter what their work entails, will have a level of knowledge about how to do their job, the organisation they work in and also specialist knowledge about products and so on. It is essential that you know what knowledge your job requires and also what knowledge you have that you use in the job or that could be useful in your working life in the future.

Experience

When you are thinking about experience do not just consider things you have done or learned at work but take into account things that have happened to you in your personal life too. Your experience could include having lived abroad, organised a charity dinner or worked with a youth group in your spare time. So, do not ignore the organisational experience you have if you have family responsibilities or the experience gained from voluntary work.

When looking at the experience you can call on in your working life, try to look at work roles you have fulfilled and broaden them out so that you do not think that you have just worked in a café, for example, but that you have worked with the public, dealt with money, worked under pressure and so on.

It is always a good idea to commit your findings to paper when carrying out an exercise like this. Although you may think you will remember everything about your own aptitudes, it is likely that you may overlook something at an important moment – such as when preparing a CV or attending an interview. Also, writing things down like this focuses the mind and a focused examination of yourself and your skills will always be better than a vague period of thinking about them. If you have listed your skills, experience, values and so on you should be able to see quite clearly just what you bring to your job and the personal resources that are in use.

If you can carry out this type of self-analysis on a regular basis it will become a habit and you will find yourself examining day-to-day actions to assess how well they went and finding out what you can do to make sure things go well next time you have to carry out that task. It is this assessment and subsequent continual improvement that is the basis of a successful programme of career development. It is part of being responsible for managing yourself.

Identifying the requirements of your work role

You can now look again at the areas of personal resources in the previous section and decide which of these are required in your current work role. Use the same categories – skills, abilities and so on – and list what you think is necessary in each category to achieve success in your current job. Use a variety of sources so that you can arrive at a comprehensive list of the job's requirements. These sources could include:

- the relevant job description
- a person specification for your job
- a discussion with your manager
- details of your last appraisal
- a review of your work diary.

In later sections in this chapter we will look in more detail at the more important categories of skills and knowledge: in Chapter 9 we will deal with values and in Chapter 7 we will see how your current work role fits into the organisation, so the details you collect at this point will be useful then. We will also look at how you can develop personally.

When compiling this list of the requirements of your work role, make sure that you do not just concentrate on the tasks that you have to carry out such as 'dealing with customers' or 'inputting data' but look also at things such as 'motivating others' or 'providing leadership'. You should aim to cover the entire job so that you know what is required of you. If you have a comprehensive picture of the job's requirements you not only see where you need to make improvements to your own skills and knowledge base but you will also develop an appreciation of the breadth of your skills and abilities that you can transfer to another job in the future.

The results of the work you do at this stage will be vital when you are discussing your job with those you report to and agreeing objectives for the role. They will also inform the direction you take in the future and help you to see how you can develop and take responsibility for managing yourself.

INSTANT TIP

If you're feeling swamped it may be because there's a lack of clarity or agreement over your job role, your manager's expectations or the absence of agreed objectives. In this case, the onus may well be on you to take the initiative to sort it out.

What knowledge do you need?

Everyone, no matter what their industry, organisation or work role will need some knowledge that is specific to the field that they are in. If you are fully informed and up to date about all the goings-on in your industry you will make better judgements in your day-to-day tasks. Industry-specific knowledge includes knowing about developments in the markets in which your organisation operates, trends in the products or services that it offers, and legislation that directly affects what the organisation does and how it does it. Neglecting this aspect of your Continuing Professional Development (CPD) is a serious mistake (more on this in Chapter 5). Your professional knowledge needs to be kept up to date so regular effort is required to add to the base of knowledge that you bring to the job.

This knowledge can be gained in several ways including:

1. On the job – you will undoubtedly pick up more knowledge about your industry and about your job as you go about your day-to-day tasks. You should always be aware that you can learn and try to grasp learning opportunities as they come along.
2. Industry-specific training resources – these could be courses that are held in-house or at local colleges or distance learning packages either via video, or online. You could also attend conferences and seminars.
3. Reading trade magazines, newsletters and online data, etc. that will give you information about your industry that is as up to date as possible.
4. Joining a professional or industry-related organisation. These organisations will often have regular magazines that are sent to you as a result of your membership, plus newsletters and meetings that will allow you to meet others in your industry.

5. Networking with others from your industry – more about this in later chapters.

When you start to work for an organisation there will usually be some sort of induction training and it may be at this point that initial gaps in your knowledge will be identified. However, as your career progresses it may also become apparent that you need to know more about specific aspects of the industry. This will depend very much on the industry and on the role that you are playing in it, but it can be difficult to identify specific gaps. It is more likely that you will have a growing sense of your lack of knowledge while you are dealing with the day-to-day aspects of your job. To identify whether or not you have a knowledge-gap problem you should be asking questions such as:

● Do people who report to you or who are on the same level as you seem to know more about the job than you do?
● Do you feel that the knowledge you brought with you into the job is becoming out of date?
● Do you want to know more about the more technical aspects of your job?
● How do you think it would help you if you read technical/trade magazines and journals related to your industry?
● Are you aware of market changes in your area of work?
● Do you ever feel that you have insufficient information to make a decision?
● Are you up to date with legislation that affects your job?

Having identified any shortfalls in your knowledge, you will need to spend some time searching out the relevant information. You may find it useful to divide your research into broad categories such as technical knowledge, knowledge of your organisation, legislation, market information, product details, and so on. Each of these types of information can be found in different ways and from different sources. Let's look at where you might find the information you need.

Type of information	Where to look
Technical	Your organisation's records or library, trade magazines, professional organisations, product literature
Knowledge of your organisation	Your organisation's website and newsletters, colleagues, your manager
Legislation	Government websites
Market	Marketing department, customers, suppliers, colleagues
Products	Marketing literature, company website, colleagues
Up-to-date industry knowledge	Networking, conversation with colleagues, current trade magazines and journals, professional organisations

Obviously, you will start your research where you have the most pressing need for knowledge. Decide which area will produce the greatest results in terms of improvement in the way you do your job. This is where you should start.

INSTANT TIP

If you use trade and professional magazines as a source of knowledge you will have to find a way of storing the information. You will find that these magazines quickly mount up and then you will not be able to find anything. So, don't leave them in a pile by your desk – either read them or file them.

While carrying out this exercise try to consider the future needs of your work role. Bear in mind that change in business today is constant. There is an ever-present need for improvement and also technology will drive further change. You will need to keep up with industry changes, changes in business trends and new technology and its uses. This need to keep up to date with change in your industry will also apply to the next section where we will look at the sorts of skills that you need to carry out your job.

What skills do you need?

Although there will be skills specific to your current role and organisation, some skills are considered to be necessary whatever job you are doing. Let's look briefly at these skills.

Communication skills

You should be able to communicate with others at all levels both verbally and in writing. This skill also covers listening. Making yourself understood and understanding exactly what you are being told is an essential skill. It is also necessary to be able to choose the appropriate method of communication. Consider the different types – you could make a phone call, send an email, write a letter, call a meeting, send a memo, set up a video conference call or discuss something with someone face to face. Some things need to be done face to face and one to one – giving formal feedback, for example, or delivering bad news – while other types of information will be easily and effectively communicated using a quick email. Finding the right method and then using the right words are essential skills in any work situation.

Numeracy and literacy

There has been a lot said in recent years about the levels of literacy and numeracy of school leavers and there is no doubt that both are essential skills at work. You should be able to read and write effectively and use numbers with confidence and if you have even the slightest lack of skills in either of these areas, you will suffer setbacks in your career as well as in health, social and domestic matters. There is a lot of help available at local colleges and online if you have any problems in these areas. In particular, many people feel slightly uncomfortable working in any detail with numbers but it is not necessary to feel like this – get help.

Ability to work in a team

This includes working as an effective member of a team and also, where appropriate, as a team leader. There is an old saying 'There is no I in team' and being an effective member of a team means playing your part in achieving a common aim. Understanding that aim and then using your own skills (there will be a wide variety of different skills in any competent team) will get better results than you could achieve alone. Being a team leader will encompass planning and project management at a basic level and these are skills that you will need as you go further in your career, so developing them now will be useful.

Don't forget that the skill of working with others will come into play in all sorts of situations in addition to working in an easily defined team. Consider how you participate in meetings for example. The people in a meeting will have to discuss matters on the agenda, reach decisions and then take action. Do you contribute sufficiently and effectively? Are you a leader or an observer? It is a skill to be successful in meetings.

Organising skills

Being able to organise yourself, others and your tasks at work will prove invaluable in whatever job you do. Being organised involves good time management and setting up effective systems to keep things on track. The ability to manage your time – and your life – by making lists, setting priorities and objectives, and creating order out of chaos, can improve your life in a number of ways. For example, you will get more done, improve your performance, reduce stress and create a better work/life balance. Learning how to get organised is usually a matter of practice and application. You can learn the basics from books (such as this one!) and from seeing how other people get more done.

Problem solving

You should be able to think constructively, plan what you are going to do about a problem and organise a solution. People who are good at problem solving are usually those who take an organised approach, defining the task, evaluating the possible solutions and then taking action. It is essential not to take action too quickly – action without proper planning and consideration of all the implications will rarely work. It is always a good idea to evaluate the process after you have implemented your solution. This will help to show you what worked and what didn't and will lead to improvements in your problem-solving skills in future.

Creative thinking

This means that you should be able to think around a situation, developing innovative solutions to problems and seeing how your performance and of others can be improved. Creative thinking can, and often does, happen by accident – while we're getting on with life and not consciously looking for solutions to problems – but some creative thinking can be done as a purposeful exercise. To develop your creative thinking skills it is important to suspend judgement while you brainstorm a solution to a problem. You should allow plenty of time to think and be careful not to rule out any ideas you may have early on in the process. Note that deliberate creative thinking involves a certain amount of risk and 'letting go'. If you have ever invented something, created a new way of looking at something or had an original idea then you are a creative thinker.

Decision making

The ability to assess a situation and reach a timely decision based on what you find is a skill that will often be used at all levels but will be especially valuable if you aspire to – or already hold – a management position. No one, not even the top business leaders that you may admire, makes the right decision every time. There are two ways of making a decision – one is using intuition (or following a hunch) and the other is evaluating evidence in a rational way. The traditional view of a talented, 'natural' business person is that he or she follows their instincts and just 'knows' what is the right thing to do while the rest of us have to use the more laborious approach to reaching a decision by assessing all our options and using lots of information and time, but in reality a blend of these two ways is almost always used.

Information technology

Essentially this is the use of computers to store, use and retrieve information and can encompass the use of a PC and other equipment such as laptops and so on. This is a skill that will, at some level, be required in all jobs. If you are in an office environment then you will usually need to be able to use a PC with confidence to produce written documents, send emails and use spreadsheets, presentation software and so on. Obviously, other jobs will require differing levels of competence and if you aspire to change careers then you will need to be familiar with the specific software that you may need to use. There are lots of ways that you can improve your information technology skills including online courses, tutorials that come with the software and courses at your local college, as well as plenty of practice in using those packages and equipment that are essential to your work role.

Interpersonal skills

Being able to deal effectively with others on a day-to-day basis is a vital skill in virtually all work roles. Even if you work predominantly alone, you will find that you will have to liaise with others from time to time and, if you are employed, you will certainly have to communicate with your boss. Of course, in roles where you will have to deal with customers, this skill assumes even greater importance. Good interpersonal skills will help you in many ways at work and in your personal life. If you develop these skills you will find it easier to work in teams and to get what you want out of meetings. They will also help you to gain promotion and to deal with responsibility when you are promoted. You will find you are better able to work effectively and collaboratively.

The ability to learn

Lifelong Learning and Continuing Professional Development are part of working life in the 21st century so a core skill for any worker is the capacity and desire to keep learning and developing your skills. If you use this capacity and desire to learn throughout your career you will undoubtedly increase your employability. Being open to learning new things is seen as an essential skill by employers in today's fast-changing world.

INSTANT TIP

If you feel that your skills fall short in any of these core skills areas, make sure that you make plans now to improve. There are plenty of courses available, or you could approach your mentor(s) for advice if you have one, or approach your manager for help. It is in the interest of any organisation to make sure that all its employees possess these core skills.

These skills will undoubtedly be useful whatever job you are doing. There are other skills that are specific to certain jobs. You may need to be able to work with a particular accounting package for example, or to be fluent in a second language. In order to list these skills you need to examine your job description in detail and also exactly what you do on a day-to-day basis. Think about what you do that someone chosen at random would not necessarily be able to do. Do you need to drive a vehicle as part of your job, for instance? And if you're managing people you will need to be able to delegate and motivate them. These are your job-specific skills.

Do you have sufficient time to carry out your job successfully?

Most people working in industry or services today will feel under a lot of pressure and will perceive that they do not have sufficient time to carry out their jobs. However, look around and you will usually find one or two people, possibly in a similar situation to yourself, who manage to get a lot more done without the panic and stress that often accompanies deadlines and pressurised working environments. These people are those who are focused and organised. They will have examined what needs to be done, set goals for themselves, and planned how and when they are going to meet those goals. People who are disorganised and who seem to be continually racing against the clock will not get as much done in each working day or achieve as much in their working lives as those who take a step back, think about what needs to be done and then approach it in an organised manner.

However, having said that people who take an organised approach will get more done, it is nevertheless the case that some people are overburdened employees. There is no doubt that we are all expected in our work roles to take on more and more, and there must be a point at which it is not possible to absorb more work. So, what can you do if you are overwhelmed by work and know that you do not have sufficient time to carry out your job successfully? First, you should tackle the issue of time management and there is more about this in Chapter 6.

When you are sure that you are managing your time as well as you can, then you must start to look at what you are expected to get through in a day. Start by writing a list of all the tasks and responsibilities that make up your work role and estimate how much time in a week or month each of the main areas takes you. Does this add up to more than your working hours? If not, then you would be well advised to keep a time log of a typical working week, noting how you are spending your time. It's useful to do this in 15 minute blocks. If you feel that you are seriously overburdened at work (or at home), the time spent on this exercise will be repaid in terms of saved time and as a learning experience that will help you to see a solution to the problem. After a week of recording in detail like this, group the main tasks together so that you will be able to see just where your time goes. What can you eliminate or cut down? Are there areas where you waste time? Having done this, you will either see where you can make changes that will help you to fit your work into the time you have or you will have some evidence that your job needs to change.

If you find that it seems impossible on paper to do everything that is involved in your work role then you will have to make changes to your job. Most changes that you may be able to make in this situation are ones that you will need to discuss with your manager. If you can make a case for job changes being necessary to make it possible to do the job in a reasonable time, then it will be your manager's responsibility to suggest and facilitate changes. However, discussions of this type always go better if you can find a solution or suggestions of your own to solve the problem before you take the problem to your boss. The idea being that you take a solution to your manager rather than just a problem.

Solutions to look at might include:

- Delegation – can you pass on some of your duties to someone who reports to you or to another department?
- Drop some tasks – are there some tasks that you are required to carry out that you consider unnecessary or duplicated?
- Do some tasks less frequently.
- Make changes within the department.
- Make changes in the way work is carried out.

The important thing, if you feel that you do not have sufficient time to do your job, is to find out why and then take steps to make the necessary changes. It is essential that you do not let the situation continue as this will lead to undue pressure and stress: taking action will not only lead to an eventual solution but it will immediately make you feel better. The problem may be the job or it may be the way you are doing it but, whichever it is, the problem must be solved.

Does your work role allow you enough time for the rest of your life?

Getting – and maintaining – a work/life balance is essential not only for your health but also to ensure that your performance at work does not suffer. If you allow work to dominate your life then you will have no time to develop or maintain relationships and a life outside work and you may start to suffer from stress with all its related symptoms. However, life at work and life at home should not be seen as competing elements, but as two parts of a fulfilling life. If one suffers then the other will also suffer.

So, how can you ensure that the time spent on your work is kept in balance with the time you need outside work? This is mainly a matter of discipline. We discuss time management in much greater detail in Chapter 6 but it is essential in terms of a work/life balance that you control your use of time both at home and at work so that you can get the most out of both your roles.

If you are sure that you are working as efficiently as possible and are managing your time effectively then your next step should be to approach your manager. He or she may be able to help in a variety of ways.

Reviewing your work role

Discussing, and perhaps revising, the content of your work role may mean that your job becomes more manageable while still ensuring that all the necessary work gets done. As we said above, it is better to take your boss a solution to the problem rather than just taking a problem to be solved, so make sure that you are very clear about what the problem is and how it can be resolved.

Training

It may be that you need training that would help you to do your job more efficiently. This may be something that you can sort out for yourself or you may need some input – possibly financial – from your employers.

Flexible working arrangements

There is a variety of flexible working arrangements that may suit different work and life situations. This can include part-time working, flexitime (where staff vary their starting and finishing times within core hour restraints so that the workplace is manned when necessary), job sharing, home working (perhaps for one or two days per week), annualised hours (where shorter hours are worked during quieter times – this is especially suitable for jobs that are seasonal), compressed hours (where you do the same number of hours as at present but over fewer days) and term-time working (this is particualrly useful to parents with young children at school). Employees who have parental responsibilities have a legal right to request flexible working arrangements, although this does not, of course, guarantee that your employer will be able to meet your needs. The employer must, however have good business reasons for refusing such a request. All other employees can, of course, request different working arrangements and many employers will look favourably on such requests as it is now generally accepted that flexible working arrangements provide benefits to both employees and employers.

INSTANT TIP

There are procedures to follow if you wish to take up your right to request that you are able to work flexibly. More details can be found at www.direct.gov.uk

Mentoring

Perhaps someone senior in the organisation could act as a mentor to you and discuss your work role with you on a regular basis to try to find ways to improve and check that you are indeed managing your time as effectively as possible. This also has the benefit of ensuring that the worker feels supported in times of stress.

The work/life balance

Your employer should have no doubts about the value of work/life balance measures such as flexible working as it is widely believed that they will produce benefits for employers such as:

- improved staff retention
- reduced absenteeism
- raised staff morale
- easier recruitment
- increased employee satisfaction
- increased productivity
- meeting legal requirements
- reduced stress in the workplace.

If you have a problem with your job taking over your life and not allowing you sufficient time to have a satisfactory life outside work then the issue must be tackled rather than ignored or accepted as 'just the way it is'. Many organisations have a culture of long working hours and this has become more prevalent in recent years. You should examine how and why you work long hours. It is always better if you measure your work by the results you achieve – your productivity – than simply by the hours you work. It is far better to work for 7–8 hours and achieve something than 10–12 hours of which 3–4 are spent chatting or on tasks that do not contribute to your goals. Analysing your working day or week so that you know exactly how you have spent all those hours at work will help.

Another way in which you can help yourself in this situation is by making sure that you have all the skills you need to do your job efficiently and effectively. This can mean asking your manager for time management training or tutorials on how to use computers more quickly for instance.

If you have a real problem and feel that work is taking over your life, you may wish to make a few rules that will help you to break the pattern of behaviour. These could include:

- Take time out during the working day – perhaps a stroll or visit to the gym at lunchtime.
- Leave work at 5pm on at least two nights per week.
- Don't take work home at weekends.
- Turn your work phone off at a certain time in the evenings.
- Say 'no' if you are being asked to do work that interferes with existing social arrangements.

A quick analysis of how much discretionary time you have in your life, i.e. time in which you can do just what you want, will help you to see if you have a good work/life balance. Your time should not be so committed that you have no choice about how you use some of it. Try making a list with the following headings:

What I must do

These are the absolutely unavoidable tasks in your life both at work and outside work such as raising invoices, contacting customers and other tasks at work, plus sleeping, eating and necessary tasks at home.

What I do not need to do

This is a difficult area. There will be things both at work and at home that you do but which could easily – or not so easily – be dropped, but which it may be difficult for you to admit, even to yourself, that you should not be doing. This might include things such as dealing with the mistakes of those who report to you at work – could they be trained not to make the mistakes, or to rectify the mistakes themselves? Or do you do things for your partner or children that they could do for themselves? Eliminating these tasks will free up time that is then discretionary time and which will make your life better in lots of ways.

What I like to do

All your hobbies belong in this category plus some tasks at work that give you satisfaction and/or enjoyment.

What I would like to do if I had the time

Let your imagination have total freedom here. If you had no calls at all on your time what would you be doing? Taking some exercise, studying something for pleasure, spending time with family and friends, travelling, watching TV, reading – whatever. Now ask yourself how much you want to do some of these things and whether the things on your list of things that you do not need to do are more important than these.

When you've completed this list, look at the balance between the four areas, especially between the things that you do not need to do and the things you would like to do. If you spend a lot of time doing things that you really do not need to do but have lots of things that you would like to do if you had the time, then some work in these areas would pay huge dividends in terms of your work/life balance and in making you feel happier and much less stressed. If you can ask yourself repeatedly as you go through life whether each thing that you do is how you should be spending your time and whether or not you can eliminate it or delegate it, you will find that you have more discretionary time than you first thought was the case – and how you use it is up to you.

The important thing to remember is that a successful working life and a satisfying life outside work are not mutually exclusive. They should be run alongside one another to ensure the success of both.

INSTANT TIP

It can cost up to twice the annual salary to recruit and train a replacement employee so if you are having problems at work, don't suffer in silence. Approach your boss, making a business case for a change to your working hours or job content.

Playing to your strengths

If you are to give your very best performance at work it is vital that you know your strengths and then use them effectively. Getting to know yourself thoroughly will take time. Of course, you will have some idea of what you are good at – but this is not necessarily the same as knowing your strengths. It will be a useful exercise in managing yourself to develop a fuller understanding of your own strengths.

Feedback analysis is a useful tool to use in determining your strengths. This is a technique that was used by – among others – John Calvin in the Calvinist Church in the 16th century. It is a long-term method of discovering your strengths so that you ensure that you place yourself in a work role that will produce growth, satisfaction and fulfilment. It entails noting your expectations of what the results will be each and every time you make an important decision or major action. After some months these expectations can be compared with actual results. Where your expectations were fulfilled or exceeded then this will pinpoint your strengths. This system can also highlight your areas of weakness – such as procrastination – that can be self-defeating.

Feedback analysis also refers to obtaining and analysing feedback from colleagues and others. Hopefully you will already get regular feedback from your manager (and if not, arrange a get together about it – now) and can use that to help you in your quest for self-knowledge. Equally important is developing a system for obtaining feedback from your peers. This should be reciprocal and will often be informal. With colleagues you can trust you will be able to get opinions on your strengths and then use this knowledge, together with the feedback from your own observations, to inform the way you work. For example, you may discover that your planning is faultless but that you are not quite so good at carrying out the actions that are necessary to bring your excellent plans to fruition.

It is essential to realise that no one can be good at everything and also that it is not usually possible to make drastic changes in ourselves. It is far better to discover our strengths and then work to them. A lot of time and energy can be wasted by trying to make major changes to remedy weaknesses when what a smart worker would do is to make the most of their strengths and then surround themselves with others who can fill the gaps in their capabilities.

Try answering the following questions to discover your own strengths:

● Decision making – or advising? Do you find decision making easy or are you able to make an organised case for something but then find it difficult to put into practice?
● Working well in groups – or alone? Some people like to be surrounded by people and will 'feed' from others, while loners are more likely to feel comfortable working unaided on a project.

- Am I a listener – or a talker?
- Am I creative – or a doer?
- Do I find technical information easy to understand – or am I better with more general information?
- Do I work well under stress – or do I need a calmer environment?
- Am I a good presenter – or better at making a written case?
- Do I perform well in a large organisation – or in a small one?
- Am I a good mentor or coach – or better at doing than teaching?
- Do I learn best by listening – or reading?
- Can I handle conflict – or do I avoid difficult situations?
- Am I a risk taker – or do I usually play safe?
- Do I handle change well – or does change worry me?
- Do I display strength of will or am I weak-willed?
- Am I confident in business situations – or am I nervous in meetings?
- Am I sensitive to people's feelings – or do I struggle to understand the problems of others?
- Do I take responsibility easily – or do I prefer to let others take the lead?

Having discovered your strengths, you should, as far as possible, put yourself in a position where you can make the most of them. Let's take the first one as an example of how this might happen. If you are a good decision maker then you can aim for the top position in any organisation or department – but you will need some people around you who are good advisers. For those responsible for managing the succession for the top job in an organisation it is essential to choose a decision maker. The person who is in the number two job may well be there because he or she is a good adviser but will not perform well if put in the decision-maker's position. So, the message is clear, discover your strengths and play to them.

Inevitably you will discover weaknesses when thinking about your strengths and there are two views of them that you can take. You can either view them as limitations or as areas to improve. Sometimes, weaknesses can also be strengths in disguise. For example, if you are a 'nitpicker' when carrying out a task and have to examine every aspect of a problem before getting on with it, it could also be seen as 'great attention to detail' – and this can be described as a strength. So, try to put a positive spin on each weakness by viewing them differently. If this seems impossible in any particular case, examine them carefully so that you can plan to tackle any necessary improvement or to minimise the effect in your daily life. Taking this positive view is essential if you are in the position of having to go for interviews.

INSTANT TIP

Everyone has weaknesses so do not be too ashamed of yours. Try to view them positively and to work out how you may be able to improve on those weak areas.

SUMMARY

We started this chapter about self-appraisal by looking at what personal resources you need to do your job. These will include skills (things we have learned) such as driving or using a piece of software, abilities (things that come naturally) such as being organised or being able to persuade others, your values (what's important to you) such as patriotism and punctuality, attitudes such as tolerance and enthusiasm, and knowledge that you bring to your job and experience – including both personal and work experience.

Next we looked at the special requirements of your work role and how these can be ascertained by examining a variety of sources including the job description, person specification and your own records of what you do on a day-to-day basis. We looked closely at the specific knowledge you need to do your job and how you can obtain it, for example, on the job, via courses, reading or networking. Keeping up with industry changes is also important to ensure future needs are met.

When we considered skills that are needed, we looked first at core skills – those that are necessary whatever job you do, i.e. working in a team, organising, problem solving, creative thinking, decision making, using information technology, interpersonal skills and the ability to learn. Next we saw that to determine job-specific skills it is necessary to examine the job description and also to look at what you do on a day-to-day basis. These skills could include things such as driving or managing and motivating people.

In the next section, we asked the question 'Do you have sufficient time to carry out your job successfully?' and found that most will feel under time pressure but that some people achieve more in their working lives because they have an organised approach. However, if you really have too much to do, the solution is to write down everything you do and see where things can be eliminated or cut down or find solutions to the problem that you can take to your boss for discussion.

We then examined the important topic of work/life balance. While not considering work and life at home as competing elements, the demands of one should not be allowed to dominate your life as this could lead to stress, poor relationships and deteriorating performance. Maintaining such a balance was seen to be a matter of discipline and of controlling the use of your time both at

(Continued)

(Continued)

home and at work, and if there are problems, approaching your boss may be useful. We also looked at strategies for breaking the behaviour patterns that can cause problems. Next, we listed examples of how we use our time in an effort to find more discretionary time in our schedules (using the headings 'what I must do', 'what I do not need to do', 'what I like to do' and 'what I would like to do if I had more time'). Next we examined how feedback can help you to discover your strengths and weaknesses and how you can obtain valid feedback from your manager and from your peers. Finding out what you are good – and not so good – at will enable you to play to your strengths and make the most of them in your job. You will also be able to work on improving weak areas when you discover them.

ACTION CHECKLIST

1. Consider your own personal resources and decide which are the most useful in your current work role.
2. What do you think would be the most productive way of increasing your industry knowledge?
3. Think about what may change in the next five years in your current organisation and industry. Will technology play a large part in those changes or have you noticed other market trends?
4. Consider how your own core skills match up to the list given in this chapter. Do you need to improve in any particular area?
5. List your own day-to-day tasks and try to eliminate or reduce the time spent on two areas of your choice.

03

How would setting objectives improve your performance?

Objectives are seen as an essential part of any planning process and are set for four main reasons:

1. They give a sense of direction.
2. They provide a target to aim at.
3. They are a means of motivation.
4. They give you something to measure your efforts against.

Without objectives, efforts are unfocused and may be wasted so it is in your best interests to set objectives. It is important to set objectives that focus on an outcome, a result, rather than just describing an activity. So, for example, you might decide to achieve a qualification by a certain date that would help your career development. Achieving a qualification is an *outcome* but booking a course would be an activity that helped you towards achieving your *objective*.

Visualising the end result as you set objectives will help you to stop procrastinating and take action. Taking action is the only way to improve. The amount of planning that goes into properly set objectives will also help you to get on with the work rather than feeling overwhelmed by the task in front of you as you would if you had not set your direction and examined all the elements of the work to be done to achieve that objective.

If you set objectives based on knowledge of where you need to improve then your performance will improve along the way to achieving those goals. At the end of the period covered by the objective it is necessary to review progress and adjust what you are doing where necessary so that performance improvement is an ongoing process.

Later in this chapter we will look at how to go about setting effective objectives but first we will see how focus and motivation, alongside objectives, can help your performance.

Focus and motivation

People who are focused and motivated are far more likely to make a success of their careers than people who simply go to work, do their jobs and come home, without ever giving anything extra to their jobs. But what is motivation? It is when you have something – such as interest or enthusiasm – that acts as an incentive and causes you to behave in a particular way. So, for example, your monthly salary could be sufficient motivation to make you go to work every day. However, there is an increasing trend towards employers requiring more from employees than just a day's work in exchange for pay. They are looking for commitment to the organisation and for their employees to do more than just follow orders. They want employees to offer solutions to problems and to think about their work roles so that they can improve performance for both themselves and for the organisation. It is quite easy to know when you are motivated. You become a far more effective worker, feel happier about going to work, are willing to give more and will usually achieve some level of success. So, how can we become more motivated?

Motivation can be defined as the psychological condition of being motivated, i.e. having a reason for action. So, in order to motivate yourself, you will need to find your own reason to work. This is, of course, easier said than done, as what motivates you may not be what motivates other people you know. Everyone comes with their own set of values (more about your values in Chapter 9) and will work according to what is important to them personally. As always, there are theories that will help to explain this. One such theory that is very popular is Maslow's 'Hierarchy of Needs'. He put forward his theory in 1943 stating that people have a list of priorities and that we would not seek to satisfy one need until we had satisfied more basic needs that were higher in priority. In order of importance his theory (as illustrated in Figure 1.1) stated that these are:

1. Bodily needs – these include hunger, thirst, warmth and sleep. These needs, it could be argued, are a starting point for working for money. If we have an income then we can keep ourselves fed, have somewhere to sleep and so on, so they do motivate us to find a job and come to work but they will probably not be enough to make us work hard towards objectives set by our bosses. If you feel that is your only motivation for doing your job, then there is probably quite a bit of work to be done on your motivation and perhaps your choice of job.

2. Shelter and safety needs – these include peace, security and stability, so our jobs will provide these to a certain extent but again, not sufficiently to seriously affect our work objectives.

3. Love, affection and belongingness needs – these include not just a loving relationship but also friendship, a sense

of belonging and social acceptance. Again, work will provide some of these needs. It may be that you are motivated by not wanting to let your colleagues down as you like to belong to a team.

4. Reputation and esteem needs – these include the need for recognition, achievement, respect and confidence. This is where your work can really satisfy a need and provide motivation in that being set a target and then reaching it will certainly give us a sense of achievement and if our achievements are rewarded then we will satisfy our need for recognition and so on. If this is an important motivating factor for you then you must make sure that your boss appreciates your need for recognition – and if he doesn't then perhaps you are in the wrong organisation for you.

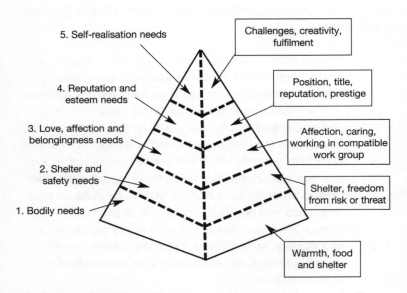

Figure 1.1 Maslow's 'Hierarchy of Needs'

5. Self-realisation needs – this means making use of our full potential. Work is an important part of satisfying this need for many people. Making full use of all our skills and abilities in our work role will fulfil this need. This motivating factor will affect your choice of career and of the organisation in which you work. It is up to you to find the right career i.e. one that will challenge you and your abilities.

Understanding what motivates us is a step towards being able to increase our motivation in any situation and although Maslow's theory does not give us a full explanation of motivation it certainly goes a long way towards helping us to understand how work can be motivating and what we should be looking for in a job and in an organisation to make sure that we are doing the best we possibly can for ourselves in our working lives. From this explanation of motivation, we can see what you will have to do to motivate yourself to work harder and to 'go the extra mile' to achieve success in your career:

● Find what gives you a sense of achievement – this will give you confidence in your own abilities, which is a key motivating factor.
● Look for satisfying work – this will increase your self-confidence.
● Take on responsibility – the recognition of being given responsibility will increase your levels of self-respect and confidence. This is why job titles are so important to some people as they see them as recognition of their abilities.
● Take every opportunity to work as part of a team – working in a cohesive, high-achieving team will satisfy your need for belonging and social interaction. Being supported by colleagues can be a hugely motivating factor in your working life.

- Look for a job, or areas in your current work role, that will challenge you and also for things that will give you scope for creativity. This will lead to feelings of fulfilment as you meet your need for self-realisation.

As you can see, motivation and the various factors that influence it in our working lives are very important. If you feel that you are not sufficiently motivated in your current work role or organisation then it is your responsibility to change your circumstances. This may mean having a conversation with your manager to try to change your day-to-day circumstances or to find a way to work towards promotion, extra training and so on. Alternatively, depending on the problems that you face, you may need to consider a move to another organisation or to change careers altogether. This requires a lot of careful thought and it would be helpful to discuss this with someone you trust.

Improving your motivation in your working life is essential if you are to make progress. Many people will feel that they are unmotivated because their employers are not doing what they should to help them but managing yourself effectively means that you must take responsibility for your own situation. A lack of motivation is easy to spot. If you or your co-workers – or the people who report to you – are unmotivated, then they will not perform effectively. There may be high rates of absenteeism and mistakes will be commonplace. This is a result of working not because you want to but because you have to.

Turning unmotivated employees – or yourself – into people who will do a good job, make a real contribution to the organisation and enjoy themselves along the way involves four main factors.

Making work interesting

While it is ideal if your manager can help with this, you can take responsibility by searching out opportunities for yourself –

volunteer for a project or look for training opportunities. Create your own challenges on a day-to-day basis by looking for ways to improve your results, to make things quicker, setting mini goals for yourself, and so on.

Making employees feel appreciated

Making a contribution is important to most people and if your manager does not make you feel appreciated, try doing it for yourself by listing all the worthwhile projects you have played a part in or all the benefits that have come to your organisation as a result of your work.

Engendering a feeling of being part of something

This can be a team, a worthwhile project or maybe simply a job well done. You can develop this feeling for yourself by making an extra effort with the people you work alongside. Try not to moan about work but use others to bounce ideas off. Seeking out like-minded individuals will help to keep your working life interesting, even when the work may be routine. You could also build this feeling of belonging by joining a professional organisation or an online forum related to your work.

Rewards

This doesn't just mean pay and bonuses. You can reward yourself when you know you have done a job well – perhaps a meal out or a small treat. Sometimes you can make this reward public so that you will get some measure of recognition for something that has produced good results. Try taking a cake in to work to share with your colleagues, announcing just what you are rewarding yourself for. Or just a mental pat on the back will often work to motivate you.

There are a number of factors which, if present, can cause a lack of motivation in a workforce including the following.

Bureaucracy

Anything that seems to hamper progress or get in the way of doing something that seems sensible can cause annoyance and general dissatisfaction.

Lack of vision

Whether trying to motivate yourself or an entire workforce, a clear vision is essential. A clear vision, communicated effectively, will act as a call to action. It can represent a challenge and is often more motivating than money or other rewards. This is one of the reasons that setting goals and objectives is so important in most work situations.

Poor working conditions

This could include things as varied as a lack of somewhere to eat, lack of cleanliness, a shortfall in training or anything that makes the working day less pleasant or rewarding.

Lack of rewards

If a proper package of rewards is not in place – pay, conditions, training, etc. – it can lead to a lack of motivation.

Relationships at work

The social element of working lives should not be underestimated. This does not necessarily mean that all the staff socialise with each other outside working hours but there should be rewarding relationships within the workplace. If there are problems between two or more members of any team then the performance of that team will suffer and all team members – not just the ones that do not get on – will suffer a lack of motivation. More serious problems such as bullying at work will certainly cause demotivation and it is the responsibility of management to deal with such issues.

Poor people management

Lack of communication and a sense of being ignored will always be demotivating to staff. If you perceive your manager as being unhelpful and perhaps feel you are not being listened to then this will lead to a lack of motivation.

Impact on personal life

If a job is seen as having a negative impact on a person's life outside work then that person may well become demotivated quite quickly. This may occur, for example, if working hours are too long or where there is a culture of staying at work until the last person has finished.

Although management must take responsibility for generally keeping its workforce motivated and productive, and for the more serious issues such as bullying at work, there is also an individual responsibility. If you feel that any of these demotivating factors are affecting you personally then you should take steps to find a solution. This may take the form of a discussion with your manager about training, for example, or taking action to ensure that you leave work on time on at least two occasions each week. You may also need to take action to plan your own development so that you have goals to aim at as this will ensure a level of motivation.

A factor closely allied to motivation is focus. Keeping your focus at work will enable you to give your best performance. Here are some tips on maintaining your focus.

Deal with distractions

This is an important part of time management (see Chapter 6 for more information on how to manage your time) but it is also important in maintaining focus during your working day. Simple things such as using voicemail rather than answering the phone continuously, controlling your environment (heat, light, noise, desk layout, etc.) and deciding your priorities for the day will enable you to maintain focus and thereby achieve your aims and increase your motivation.

Set deadlines

In the next section we will deal with setting objectives but, in addition to your main objectives, you should have a series of smaller 'mini-goals' that will ensure your progress throughout the working day and will help to keep you focused and motivated.

Focus on the benefits

It is impossible for all the tasks that you have to do to be really interesting and to engage your full attention. However, if you are able to see why you are doing something and what the benefits of doing it are then it is easier to keep going.

If you can maintain focus at work then you will be far more likely to achieve your aims and this will, in itself, be hugely motivating. Improving both your focus and your motivation in your working life will improve how you feel on a day-to-day basis and is your responsibility.

Setting SMART objectives

As we saw earlier, setting objectives can improve your performance significantly both at work and in your personal life – but they must be the right objectives and set in the right way. One test of whether your objectives are going to be productive for you in terms of improvement is to ensure that they are 'SMART'. This acronym usually means that they will be Specific, Measurable, Achievable, Realistic and Timed, but sometimes means other things such as 'agreed' instead of 'achievable'. Let's look at each of these in a bit more detail.

Specific

It is important not to be vague when setting objectives. The way the objective is stated is important. It must be concrete and detailed so that there is no doubt as to what the objective is setting out to achieve. It is useful to ask questions about the objective and if any of them are unanswered then it is likely that the objective is not specific enough. Ask questions such as:

- What needs to be done?
- Why am I doing this?
- Who will do the work?
- When will this be completed?
- How am I going to do this?

An example of a poorly set goal in this respect would be 'I must improve the sales figures.' This would be a better goal if set so that it is more specific – try 'I will improve sales by 10 per cent by the end of the year by increasing the number of sales calls I make.'

Measurable

How will you know when the objective has been met? There is a saying that 'if you can't measure it, you can't manage it' so you need to be clear as to how you will measure progress towards your objective and also know when the objective has been met by reaching some measurable target.

It is a good idea to set milestones along the way to your objective so that you will be able to measure the progress you are making and stay on track. This not only ensures that you meet your objective on time but also acts to motivate you, increasing your chances of success.

Keeping with the example of the two goals as set out above, the first, poorly set goal is not measurable. If your goal is to improve sales then you need to answer the questions 'By how much?' and 'By when?' so that at the end of the period you are able to see quite clearly whether or not the goal has been achieved.

Achievable

Make sure the objective set is achievable given the skills and resources you have at the time. Resources can include money and management support as well as time and the right people and equipment. You should also take into account any constraints imposed in a work situation. Note that if an objective is not completely achievable you may lose motivation and then achieve nothing. So, for example, if your organisation is unable to dedicate any extra resources to its sales efforts, don't set your sales objectives too high.

Realistic

Don't think that this means all your objectives must be modest. You can set your sights high and yet still have a realistic objective. If you truly believe you can do it, then it is realistic. Of course, even a realistic objective will require effort from you and may also need a change of your personal priorities.

Keeping goals realistic is important, so don't say you will achieve a 100 per cent increase in sales if the best you have ever done in previous years is a rise that was in single figures. The 10 per cent stated in the example above would be much more realistic even though it could still be said to be ambitious in the circumstances.

Timed

When do you want to achieve your objectives? Be specific about the timescale so that it is not allowed to drift and then is possibly never achieved at all because there is no set time for it.

The example above sets a time limit of 'the end of the year' so this fulfils the need to know when the goal must be achieved.

If your objective is written down, following the SMART criteria, then there is a far greater chance of success than if an objective is a vague idea in your head with no time limits and no clear idea of who will do the work and how it will be done. So get SMART with your objectives.

In most organisations you will have the opportunity to discuss your work role with those you report to and to agree personal work objectives. While you are considering and setting your objectives it is important that you also work out how you will measure progress towards those objectives and this is detailed in forthcoming sections. But before that, we will look at how you should set goals that will be achieved in the short term and also ones for the long term.

Setting long-term and short-term goals

As the name suggests, short-term goals are ones that we expect to achieve over a short period of time – say a week or a month – whereas long-term goals reach further into the future and may be something we are aiming to achieve in a year, five years or even 20 years.

Long-term goals often encompass our dreams and are the most meaningful of our objectives. However, the timescale of such goals may be off-putting to us. It may be difficult to maintain our focus and motivation over a period of years. For this reason, we should ensure that we work towards our long-term goals with a series of short-term goals – these are also known as enabling goals. These will follow the steps you need to take to achieve the long-term goal and also help to keep you motivated and on track with a positive attitude. For example, you may have a long-term goal of achieving promotion to Creative Director either in your current organisation or in another. To do this you may need to gain extra qualifications and to build up your CV by taking on – and making a success of – a variety of projects. Your short-term goals in this case would then include gaining access to the courses you need to take and then passing them to attain the qualifications you need. You would also need to develop your work role so that you have gained the right experience, worked on the right projects and got to know the right people and information so that your CV becomes one that would impress those looking to appoint a Creative Director.

The two main elements that you need to be aware of when deciding what your goals are to be are commitment and goal conflict. If you do not have sufficient commitment to any particular goal it is likely that it is not a real goal but is simply a dream. If you are not prepared to be committed to a goal by putting in the effort that is necessary to achieve it, then you should rule that out of your list of goals. It is demotivating to have a goal that you never achieve. Often the goals to which you do not show sufficient commitment are not set with the SMART principles in mind. Such goals will be vague ('I'd love to lose weight', for example) and will have no timescale set for them ('I'd like to be rich one day'). In setting your goals you should also be aware of goal conflict. If two of your goals are in conflict with each other then it is unlikely that you will achieve either of them so you will need to drop one – or both – of them. An example of this type of conflict would be wanting to earn a high salary while at the same time aiming to work in the charity sector. You would be unlikely to get a high-paying position in this sector, so even if you are offered a job working for a charity it is possible that you would not accept it because of the goal conflict.

An example of long- and short-term goal setting in the workplace occurs in a sales environment where short-term objectives would achieve higher sales in, say, a year and other goals to improve sales could be set within a longer timeframe.

So, short-term goals to improve sales to be achieved in one year might include:

- increased profit margin per average sale
- an increase in quantity of product sold
- a number of new customers per month per sales representative
- geographical expansion
- new product launch.

Note that to be effective these goals would have to be stated in more specific terms according to individual circumstances.

And long-term goals to achieve the same objective could include:

- expand into export markets
- a new brand launch
- new strategic sales alliances with other organisations
- reduction of returns and complaints by setting up new departments and processes
- reduction of sales personnel.

As always – whether long-term or short-term – goals should be SMART as detailed in the previous section. Care when setting goals and also thinking strategically should ensure a greater chance of success.

Measuring progress against your objectives

Having set your goals and objectives – both long-term and short-term – it is vital that you keep track of your progress towards them. Measuring progress towards your objectives will serve three purposes:

1. It will keep you on track – if you are letting anything slip in your quest for success, it is far better to know when things are going wrong along the way rather than getting to the end of the project and finding that the objective has not been met. It will allow you to adjust your plans and take steps to correct what has gone wrong.
2. It will motivate you to keep going – just knowing that you are making progress and seeing some solid signs of it are immensely motivating and will ensure that you keep your focus.
3. The people you report to will be able to measure your progress. You can then agree a development plan and work towards improvement.

Measuring your progress can be made easier by ensuring that you set objectives that are measurable and which have a series of 'mini-goals' along the way. Monitoring your progress towards your ultimate goal is essential for the reasons stated above and can be done without too much effort if the objectives are set with measurement in mind.

It is useful to create a timeline against which you can plot your progress as you go along. All measurement requires some collection of data, so systems for this must be set up at the start of any improvement plan. Regular deadlines must be created so that work is not allowed to progress for too long in the wrong direction or to get too far behind schedule. These deadlines should be spaced out as appropriate throughout the life of the project. So, for example, a project that is expected to last a year could have milestones at quarterly intervals but a shorter task could have milestones set much closer together. A regular programme of reviews can then be carried out and corrective action taken as appropriate if problems are detected.

Sometimes, however, we set goals where the objectives are clear but how to measure progress towards these objectives is not obvious. Career goals can often fall into this category. Let's take an example to illustrate how this problem can be overcome. Suppose you have set yourself a goal of achieving promotion to the equivalent of your manager's job in three years. At first this might seem that until you get to the end of the three years you will not know if you are on track or making any progress towards it. The way to overcome this is to evaluate what you need to do to get there and then to set goals along the way. So, for example, you may find that you need to gain experience of making presentations and to obtain membership of a professional organisation. You can set goals for attaining these 'mini-goals'. You could decide that you will have given three major presentations in your organisation (or outside, perhaps in a voluntary capacity) by the end of the first year. This could involve finding the opportunities to give presentations by making it known to your boss that you would welcome such occasions, as you feel you need to improve in this area, or by offering to help with a major project.

Putting yourself forward is one way that you can ensure progress towards a goal of this kind. With regard to the professional qualification, you could set a time limit for when you will have found out exactly what you have to do to achieve this and then another target for completing the course and so on.

Then, in the final year before your ultimate goal, you could start to research and apply for the kind of positions that you are aiming at. With a three-year objective like this you could measure your progress after six or 12 months – have you completed the set number of presentations, or researched the qualifications by the required date? If not, why not? What can you do to push towards your objective?

Remember that your objectives must also be closely linked with the objectives and activities of the organisation for which you work so, when assessing progress, you must take into account any changes that have taken place within the organisation and consider the effect these changes may have on your objectives. Organisational changes could affect the validity of the objectives so that some directional change is needed or it may be that your personal circumstances are affected by the way the organisation has changed and your objectives must be amended to take this into account.

Regularly evaluating how you have performed against your objectives will reinforce your actions and, if you act on what you find, will ensure that you continue to improve your performance. Evaluation should include finding the answers to questions such as:

● Has the objective been achieved?
● Has it been achieved on time?
● If not, why not?
● Do you think you could have done more?
● What problems did you encounter?
● Did you identify any skills gaps?
● How do you feel about your objectives now?
● Are your objectives still appropriate, given any changes in circumstances?

The task of evaluating how you have performed against your objectives can be made easier and usually more productive by discussing it with someone else. If the goals are related to your work role, such as those objectives agreed at an annual appraisal for instance, then your manager is obviously the best choice and this should be done as a matter of course if they have been involved in setting the objectives. But if setting the objectives was a personal exercise carried out for your own purposes and aimed at personal development then your options might include:

● your boss – getting their opinion will almost always help if your ultimate aim is career progression
● a friend or relative – if they know you well and you feel you can trust their opinion and discretion, then this could be a wise choice
● a colleague – the proviso above about trust and discretion applies here too

- a mentor
- a career counsellor.

The aim of such discussions and evaluation is to assess your progress towards your goals and to start the planning process for future objectives.

As always, information is useless unless action is taken. If you identify a skills gap during the evaluation of your objectives, for example, your next set of objectives should include action to rectify this. Also, you should take advantage of the lessons you will have learned about yourself and your organisation. You may have discovered that you performed better than you expected or that there is a system deficiency in your organisation. Do not ignore what you have learned but take action to ensure that you benefit in some way from your efforts. Even when you have met your objectives there are lessons to be learned and further improvements to be made. You will be able to fine-tune your skills and to continue your development.

It is a good idea to keep a record of your objectives, your measures of success and the results of your efforts. Even if this is the first time that you have set personal goals and objectives, you will not have just one set of objectives in your working lifetime – your priorities, needs and your situation will change as you go through your career. Seeing how your objectives change over the years can be an interesting exercise in itself but recording what you have achieved against those objectives will be beneficial in terms of motivating you for the future and informing the goals that you will set. (There is more about updating your goals and objectives in the next section.) It can also be useful to record the reasons why you have not met your goals. Indeed this can be one of the more productive aspects of the exercise as it will help you to decide whether or not the objectives were correct for you or where your efforts fell short of what you expected. Obstacles that got in the way of achieving can be examined and action taken to avoid them in the future. Also note where targets were met – were they too easy? This could be an opportunity to set more challenging goals for yourself that will really push you to be the best that you can be. Reviews like this are all part of the improvement process.

Anyone who doubts the value of measuring progress towards objectives in this way should remember the anonymous quote 'What gets measured, gets done.'

Achieving your goals

The key to meeting your objectives on time and on budget is planning. This can be more difficult than actually carrying out the actions necessary to achieve your goals but it is a vital part of the process. Planning will help you to bring together the various elements of your goals. Ask yourself questions such as:

- Do I have the resources? Make sure that you plan when you will have the time available to carry out the work and that other resources such as money and equipment are in place.
- Are other people involved and, if so, are they on board? Plan to make sure that others involved are informed of the objectives and fully aware of what is required of them.
- What else will be happening during the period covered by the objectives? Plan for other major projects that you may have scheduled and also for holidays as these can throw your plans off track. Other calls on your time may well demotivate you and make your objectives much more difficult to achieve.
- Can I add in more milestones? Having a number of points in your plan where you will know whether or not you are on track will, as we have already said, assure a greater chance of success and keep you going to the end.

- Have I plotted a clear, sensible route to the objectives? Double checking will always help to make sure you're doing things correctly.

Planning will give your objectives a clear focus and show you just where you are going. It will vastly increase your chances of success.

Updating your work goals and objectives

Your objectives should be subject to regular review. It is not usually possible to set out your objectives then leave them unchanged for years to come as things will change along the way. Your interests or your family circumstances will change, for instance, and then you may need to change direction in your working life. There will almost inevitably be some sort of reorganisation or other changes within your company that may affect your objectives.

The trend now is for people to have a number of careers in their working life rather than, as was the case a few decades ago, for someone to decide what they wanted to do when they left school or university and continue doing that work until they retired. One of the reasons for this is changes in the economy that have affected job security. Another reason is the increasing demand for choice in all areas of our lives. Many people have been made redundant from one job and have seen it as an opportunity to start on another path. Increasingly, people of all ages are starting small businesses or retraining long after they have left school or university. All of this means that the objectives decided upon in your twenties or thirties will not suffice for the rest of your working life, so regular reviews have become even more important.

Conducting a review of work objectives entails a thorough examination of all the elements of your goals. Ask yourself questions such as:

- Have there been changes in the organisation that affect the objectives?
- How far have I progressed towards my objectives?
- Are my objectives still feasible?
- Am I satisfied with the way my working life is developing?
- What do I want to change in my working life?
- Have my personal circumstances changed since I last reviewed my objectives?
- Have my values changed?
- Have my interests changed?
- Could I have pushed myself harder and achieved more?

When you have answered these questions you will know whether or not major changes to your objectives are required. There are two aspects to this. First, if the objectives have been agreed with the people you report to and there are problems with the progress you are making towards them, then they will want to agree appropriate action to get you back on track. Second, your personal development plan may be affected. If you feel that you are on the right path for you, then you will be able to make only minor changes and continue on that path. However, if you want to go in a different direction then you will need to go back to the beginning of the goal-setting process. Reviews of your objectives will ensure that they remain fit for purpose and that you can recognise the changes and adjust your plans accordingly.

A major reason why reviews of work goals become necessary is that you can become bored and stale in a job. If this is the case it is essential that you do not stay where you are simply because you cannot see another path, or because it is expected of you, or because you are frightened to change. If you are no longer as interested in your chosen path as you once were, then you should review your goals and make the changes. There are a number of areas that you should examine to check if the job is still right for you.

Have your interests changed?

For instance, you may have been passionate about accountancy when you were in your teens and twenties but if it bores you now then you need to find something that really interests you. It could be teaching, the law or something artistic but the important thing is to find it and recognise that it is never too late to make a change.

Does the money matter?

Of course, the vast majority of us work for money but sometimes our needs change and we may need more or less than we did when we took the job. The questions that you need to ask yourself at this stage are does the money you receive justify the work and effort you put into this job and is it sufficient for your current needs? Negative answers here indicate a change is needed.

Is your job a challenge?

For some people challenge is all-important while for others they have enough to think about in their personal lives so they're not looking for more challenge at work. Make your decision for yourself and change your career objectives if necessary.

Are you satisfied?

If you are feeling dissatisfied with your job then you need to find out why. If you find that there is very little that you can do to increase your job satisfaction in your current position then this will signal the need for major changes. It may be that you need to completely rethink your career and your objectives. Do you need to change professions, retrain or go back to education?

There are a number of changes that can alter your perception of your job or your career and therefore cause your objectives to need a review. These include:

- a change of boss
- the company being taken over or merging with another
- reorganisation within the company
- redundancies
- your job responsibilities being changed
- your home responsibilities changing.

Whatever the reason for the change, regular reviews will keep your objectives up to date and relevant.

What if you don't achieve your goals?

If your goals are right for you and for your situation, you plan effectively and work hard then it is extremely likely that you will achieve them. But no one can control everything in their lives and the unexpected can – and does – happen. However, not meeting goals should not be a reason to despair, become demotivated or to abandon future goals. If this is a situation that you find yourself in then it should be viewed as a learning opportunity. Better to try and fail than not try at all. Let's look at some of the reasons why goals are sometimes not met.

Excuses

Let's rule these out first. Blaming other people will get you nowhere and being a victim of circumstance is no reason for not trying to improve.

Ignoring other things that are going on around you. When you are planning what you need to do to achieve your objective you must take into account other things that demand your time and other resources. This also applies to other people who are vital to your objectives. You cannot commit their time without consulting them.

Changes

To be successful you have to accept that things will change during the time that you are working on your goals, especially if the timescale for achieving your objective is long. You must deal with changes as they come along and revise your actions as necessary. Milestones during the project will help you to see the effect of changes.

Targets that were too high

Remember that goals must be achievable and realistic.

Lack of effort

Setting goals is not an end in itself. You have to put in the effort that is necessary to reach your goals. There is no substitute for hard work.

Lack of planning

There is a saying 'Failing to plan is planning to fail' and it is very true. Setting objectives then not planning how to reach them will not allow you to improve at all.

Unrealistic timescales

Again, note that objectives must be SMART – Specific, Measurable, Achievable, Realistic and Timed.

Lack of understanding

Make sure that you are aware of all the ramifications of what you are doing. Taking into account the overall goals of the organisation and being aware of what is going on around you when you are setting your objectives will help with this.

Lack of communication

If others are involved, they must fully understand what is required of them and when. If you do not communicate this clearly, then failure is more likely.

Too few milestones

If you have sufficient milestones along the way towards your ultimate goal you will be able to see when things are not on track and then put things right so that you do reach your goal.

Having examined the reasons why you might not achieve your goals, let's look at what you can do in this situation. The first thing to say is that you should not, under any circumstances, allow yourself to become disheartened and to give up. Improvement can be a gradual process, with perhaps some giant leaps forward from time to time and very slow progress at others, and you will only improve if you keep trying and learning from your experiences. If you have not met your targets then a more detailed review is necessary. You will need to determine what progress you made on the way to your deadlines and find out specifically what went wrong – and what went right.

Your examination of your progress should encourage you to set new goals and keep trying to improve. Be especially careful to set the right goals in this case and to set as many short-term goals and milestones as you can so that you will see progress more easily. You will then be able to adjust your goals according to what happens along the way. This will probably also be a good time to enlist some help. If you have a mentor, arrange a meeting to discuss what you should do next and how you can improve. If your goals are part of your work role then you should certainly have detailed discussions with your manager. Your aim is to improve continually so set new goals and then carefully plan how you can achieve them. It is always helpful if you can come to view failure as an opportunity to learn and improve,

SUMMARY

In this chapter we discussed how setting objectives could improve your performance. There are four ways they can help – by giving a sense of direction, providing a target and motivation, and by giving you something to measure your results against.

Next we looked at focus and motivation. Motivation is something that acts as an incentive, causing you to act in a particular way, i.e. having a reason for action. Maslow's Hierarchy of Needs helped to explain this. This theory says that we seek to satisfy our needs in order of importance ranging from bodily needs, to shelter and safety, love and belongingness, reputation and esteem to self-realisation needs. Having found out more about what motivates us, it is the individual's responsibility to motivate themselves and ways to do this were discussed including making work interesting, feeling appreciated, becoming a part of something, reducing bureaucracy and improving working conditions. Focusing on the benefits of your work can help with motivation.

Next we discussed how to set SMART objectives – Specific, Measurable, Achievable, Realistic and Timed. Goals should be set for the long term and the short term and we examined how these can both be useful. Then we looked at the importance of measuring progress against objectives so that you will keep motivated, on track and work towards continuous improvement. Evaluating your performance against objectives is also essential so that future development can be planned.

How to achieve your goals was discussed next including checking that resources are available, setting milestones and taking other people and events into account. Following this, further objectives can be set, noting changes in personal and job circumstances. Finally, we looked at the reasons why you might not meet your goals and what you can do in the future to increase your chances of success.

ACTION CHECKLIST

1. Consider your own objectives – are they SMART?
2. Assess your objectives – to what extent do they motivate you?
3. Are you clear about exactly what motivates you? Check Maslow's theory and see where your job comes in his scale of motivating factors.
4. Using the objectives you are currently working towards, check what milestones you have reached – are you on target for success?
5. If not, why not? Look at the reasons given in this chapter and assess which have affected you.

04

How can you fill any gaps in your current skills?

In order to move forward with your career and, indeed, in life in general, it is necessary to develop and learn. Some development will take place whether this is something you are focused on or not. As we go about our daily lives things happen that change our views or expand our spheres of interest and we learn as we go along. If all our development is this type of natural learning and changing we will not achieve our full potential. Consider someone who never goes anywhere new, doesn't meet new people and keeps to the same activities that they have had for years. That person will still be living a life but will not have many new ideas and there will be no progress towards any improvements in life. To improve we have to be proactive and ready to embrace new ideas, people and activities.

To make real progress we need to focus on our own personal development. This is especially true in our work lives. Your aim in focusing on personal development to improve your prospects at work must be to fill any gaps in your skills and also to undertake more general activities that will 'round out' your personality and make you more useful to employers. Developing yourself with this aim can be as simple as reading relevant work-related material, meeting people working in your industry or taking a course. To improve your current skills base you must first identify gaps in your current skills, and then concentrate specifically on filling those gaps.

Identifying gaps

First it is important to understand what a skills gap is. It is when your actual capabilities and the required capabilities of your current or future work role are different. The difference is the skills gap. Analysing this gap obviously requires a depth of knowledge of both yourself and of the job that you do – or would like to do.

There are a number of skills that are considered to be core job skills i.e. those skills that most jobs with any degree of responsibility will require, and they will be the skills that are absolutely vital if you are to look at career progression. These include, as we discussed in Chapter 2, communication skills, numeracy and literacy, the ability to work in a team, organisation skills, problem solving, creative thinking, decision making, interpersonal skills, an ability to use information technology and the ability to learn throughout life. If you identify any lack of these core skills in yourself, take steps straight away to rectify the situation. Without these core skills you will be at a disadvantage in any work situation. Any time, effort and money you can put in to improve these skills will not be wasted.

There will also be skills that are specific to the job you are doing – or the job you would like to be doing in the future. So, next you should examine the specific job requirements to identify these skills. In most organisations there will usually be a job description and possibly also a person specification that will outline the skills requirements of that particular work role. This is normally produced to help interviewers and managers when they are trying to find the right person for the job and will tell you what you need to know about the job's requirements. It will usually be split into a number of areas such as:

- qualifications
- experience
- skills and aptitudes.

If, when you have assessed your own attributes, you find that you lack the relevant qualifications then it will be a straightforward process to find the courses that will fill this gap. Experience is a more difficult gap to fill and will take time and a planned approach. You will need to take on jobs and projects specifically to gain the experience you need. If your gaps are found to be in the area of skills and aptitudes then this is where personal development will help you most.

If the work role you are assessing is one that you aspire to in the future then defining the job's requirements may be more difficult. You will need to research the job and possibly enlist some help from your manager or people with relevant work experience. When you have a list of the requirements of a job that you would like to have in the future you will be able to compare this list with your own skills, attributes and qualifications (there will be more about this in this section) to identify any gaps. In this case you will probably have more time to fill the gaps and will need to make a plan with each gap forming an objective in your plan.

Next you need to understand and define your own skills, capabilities, experience and qualifications. A good starting point is your most up-to-date CV. If it is some time since you updated your CV then it will be a really useful exercise to write a new one. Next you need to add to it as much as you can about yourself. Most CVs are, by necessity, kept brief and to the point. They will be tailored to a specific job application and will be only a starting point for this exercise of understanding what skills and capabilities you have. At this point you should be expanding your CV into a much wider document that includes skills, aptitudes and attitudes you may have such as report writing, dealing with people, punctuality, attention to detail, drawing, sewing or sports. This will require some thought to make sure you do not miss anything and is worth spending some time on. Don't worry that some of your skills seem a bit trivial – your next task will be to make them more work related. For example, being a sporty person may mean that you have strength and stamina or maybe your drawing skills point to a creative ability, all of which could be essential skills in specific jobs. Also, don't forget less tangible aspects of yourself such as being confident, open to change or being a generous, giving person.

When you have a completed document that describes you and your capabilities you will be able to compare it with a job description and person specification and see just where the gaps are.

INSTANT TIP

You can get some ideas about the skills that employers are looking for in particular jobs by scanning the job adverts in newspapers or online.

Although this sort of exercise will take you a long way towards understanding your skills and capabilities, it will not do the whole job and it may be useful for you to ask yourself a few questions to tease out where your gaps are. Try asking – and answering – the following:

● Do I know enough about my organisation – who is in charge, its aims and values, for instance?

- Do I know enough about the technical aspects of my job? Is my knowledge up to date?
- Do I make decisions easily and quickly?
- Do I act on my own initiative or do I follow instructions?
- Do I find it easy to get my point across?
- Am I comfortable when dealing with other people?
- Do I think quickly at work?
- Do I generate new ideas and solutions?
- Am I proactive?
- Do I manage my time well or am I always racing against time?
- Do I get feedback from others around me at work and if so, what do they say?

The answers to these questions will help you to understand what needs to be done to ensure your continuing development. Some areas will undoubtedly stand out as in need of improvement and you should start with these when you are looking to learn and develop. At this point it is a good idea to set yourself some goals. Decide where you need to improve and set a goal that will address that need and give it a deadline. There is more about goal setting in Chapter 3.

Having identified where your gaps are you will need to fill those gaps. This is done by developing and learning, which is what we look at in the next section.

Ways to learn and develop

At this point you may be wondering why you need to develop and why it must be planned. This is connected with your motivations – what makes you tick, whether or not you are happy where you are or whether you want to progress. If you chose progression for yourself then you will need to devote some time to developing yourself on a personal and work basis. There may be several reasons for your desire for development and learning at any given time. These could include:

- You are feeling bored and dissatisfied with your current position.
- You are aiming at long-term career progression.
- You want to keep up with change.
- You have identified a skills gap.
- You or your employer has identified skills that you will need in the future.

It is easier first to consider general development as this can be carried out by everyone and is not job-specific. Rather than filling gaps to equip you for a work role, general development will give you less specific skills. Activities you can undertake to ensure your general development throughout life include travelling, becoming independent in areas such as making arrangements or cooking, or general experiences that are outside your normal routine. If you are open to new experiences and have a real desire to improve yourself at home and at work then your chances of success in any field will be much higher than if you left everything to chance. Taking the easy way out – saying you haven't got time to take on development activities – is almost the same as saying you can't be bothered.

Next we move on to developing in specific areas that are tailored to a particular work role. The activity you will undertake here obviously depends on the gap that you are trying to fill but there are broad categories of activities to fill the different types of gap, as shown in the following table.

Gap	Activity
Lack of qualifications	Training courses
Basic knowledge and information	On-the-job training and your own research, reading, etc.
Practical skills such as IT skills or speaking another language	On-the-job training or a course
Missing attributes such as lack of confidence	Mentoring or coaching
Creative thinking	Idea generating exercises – alone or in a group

There are lots more ways to learn and develop and these will have to be chosen to suit the particular gap that you are trying to fill but the details above will give you a start as to what you should be doing. Your employer will probably be able to help.

Let's look now at the variety of activities you can undertake in order to learn and develop. These could include:

- on-the-job training
- cross-training (i.e. learning about other jobs in the organisation)
- in-house training courses
- external courses
- attending conferences and seminars
- membership of a professional organisation
- online courses
- development projects
- shadowing someone in another department
- mentoring
- coaching

- correspondence courses
- job rotation
- brainstorming in your team
- reading self-help books and/or technical literature.

As you can see, there are lots of different activities you can undertake and you may want to try several of them. You will no doubt find that some suit you better than others and that some serve your particular needs better. The timescales involved in the various methods will also have to be taken into account. If you have an immediate need to obtain some knowledge then there will be little point in your undertaking a three-year course to find it, but you will probably find that reading about the subject or obtaining advice from a mentor will serve your purpose much more effectively.

Developing your skills in a particular area is straightforward to do once you have identified where your development needs are. Reading around the subject that you need to improve on will always help, as will meeting and talking to people in the know.

Finally in this section, remember that you should always try to enlist the help of your manager in any examination of your development needs as not only may they be able to help you to find the training you need but may also be able to pinpoint the gaps in your skills and experience. A manager will usually be able to offer training opportunities such as in-house and on-the-job training, participation in special projects and cross-training. He or she/your boss may be able to introduce you to influential people from whom you can learn or let you attend meetings or join teams that will give you a wealth of experience. And, of course, they may be able to organise the finance for a variety of training methods. Do not worry that managers will not help you if your career aims could take you outside your current organisation as, in the current climate, this will be quite common and the important thing is that you are loyal to your company right now. Generally, it is not possible for people's career plans to be completely devoted to one organisation – very often they must move to improve and this is usually accepted.

A further obstacle you may face in asking your manager to provide training for you is the common excuse of 'lack of funding'. Some organisations are very liberal with their training budgets, even in a difficult economic climate, because they appreciate the added value a competent member of staff can bring to the organisation but others will be resistant to spending on something from which they cannot see an immediate return and they will point to the fact that the newly-trained employee may leave. The way to counter this is to use the old adage: 'If you think it's a waste to develop staff only for them to leave, imagine what will happen if you fail to train staff – and they stay!' You could also point out the recognised benefits of developing staff, including:

- better staff retention
- the organisation becoming more competitive
- greater flexibility among staff
- greater motivation.

So, don't just accept an employer's resistance to offering training. There are benefits both for you as an individual and for the organisation as a whole, and if the organisation you currently work for refuses to help to develop staff, then perhaps it is not the right one for you.

Could a mentor help you in your development?

The purpose of mentors is to assist in development by providing guidance and support. They can be helpful at all stages of your career, whether you are at the start of your career and need help in deciding what you should be doing to reach your potential, or further on in your career and wrestling with a particular problem or have run out of ideas about what you should do next to develop your career.

Developing a close relationship is essential to the success of mentoring so it is not usually something that happens overnight. Your mentor(s) can be someone who works in the same organisation as you or someone not connected with it. They will usually, however, be someone senior to you so that they will have plenty of work and life experience to bring to the relationship.

So, how can you go about finding a mentor? First you need to decide just what you need from a mentor. Look at the following possible benefits the relationship – or mentors – may bring you:

- general career guidance
- a sounding board
- industry and business knowledge
- advice on how to get a new job
- training and development advice
- support when the going gets tough.

It may help to consider what help you have had from people in the past. This will develop your thoughts about mentoring in two ways. First, it will help you to see what sort of help is useful to you and second it will guide you in your search for a mentor. Could one of the people who have helped you in the past be a mentor to you now? Or perhaps you can see what sorts of people can be helpful to you and this may guide your search. Having examples like this can be extremely useful. It may also help to discuss this on an informal basis with a friend or perhaps your manager so that you can bring your ideas together and take note of any helpful suggestions they may have. At this point, a list of your possible mentors should be emerging and you will need to prioritise it. Next you need to think about how you would summarise what you think you need from a mentor. This summary will be useful when you are approaching anyone whom you think could mentor you.

So, you've got a prioritised list of possible mentors and a good idea of what you are looking for and you must approach the first person on your list. Don't be coy, call and ask them if they can spare you a few minutes to talk about your career. Make sure you make it clear that you respect them and have approached them because of their reputation/business experience/helpfulness/ approachability, etc. and also that you appreciate that they are very busy and you do not want to take up too much time. You don't want people to feel cornered from the beginning of the relationship. If they really cannot (or are unwilling to) spare the time then they are not an ideal mentor for you and you must move on to the next person on your list.

During your meetings with possible mentors repeat that you respect them and value their experience and so on, and explain from the outset what sort of help you are looking for. With luck your chosen mentors will respond positively to your requests and lasting, invaluable relationships will be formed.

When you have found suitable mentors, there are several rules to follow in your dealings with them.

Confidentiality

You should be able to confide in your mentor and be sure that it will not go any further. If you do not feel this trust in a mentor you will not have the full and open relationship that will get the best out of you. You need to be able to divulge your wildest dreams or discuss your most traumatic problems and be sure that you will not be judged. You need to be safe in the knowledge that what you discuss will not reach the ears of your boss or anyone in your organisation.

You should be in charge

If you are being mentored then you must drive the relationship. It is up to you to find your mentor(s) and then to make it clear what sort of help you need. You must be the one to put the effort in.

Set firm guidelines

How often will you meet? And where?

Take action

If your mentor suggests something you can do to improve, do it.

Manage your expectations

While you must make it clear what you want from the relationship, you cannot expect your mentor to work miracles. Your life will not change overnight and you will have to do a lot of work to put your mentor's advice into practice.

Keep track of your progress

Discuss how you will measure the effect of taking action on your mentor's advice and make sure you keep them informed of any improvements you make as a result.

Finally, don't forget to thank anyone who helps you in any way.

Building a personal development plan

In this book there is a great deal of discussion and thinking for you to do regarding assessing your own skills and attributes, your values and your goals. All of this will add to your personal and career development. A lot of what happens in anyone's career is about being in the right place at the right time with the right aptitudes and qualifications. But do not think that this is simply good luck or accident. The more you plan and develop, the better your chances of things going as you want them to, rather than things just happening to you. For this reason you should be prepared to spend quite a bit of time and effort on personal development and on thinking about yourself and your career. Not only will this ensure your advancement and meeting your goals in life but it will also be part of your Continuing Professional Development (CPD), which is a requisite in many organisations and is part of membership of many professional associations. For this reason, as well as keeping yourself organised, you should keep a record of all the personal and career development activities you undertake. Building your plan and carrying out the activities that will lead to a comprehensive plan with good chances of success is your responsibility – although you are very likely to get help from your employer if you ask.

An organised approach to personal development is essential, so you will need a plan to help you to fill the gaps in your skills, knowledge and capabilities that you have identified. It will also help you to see where you are going in terms of your career and your life as a whole.

A lot of gaps can be filled by experience so build that into your plan if you can by looking for opportunities at work. You should also take every opportunity to reflect on what has gone well – and not so well – so that you can learn that way.

Your plan, as always, will be more effective if it is written down and reviewed on a regular basis. An example of how such a plan might look is as follows:

Skill needing development	Actions to be taken	When to be completed
Conversational French	Find and book a course	3 months
	Find someone to practise with	3 months
Presentation skills	Look for opportunities to practise presenting	12 months
	Become more proficient with PowerPoint© by practising at home	3 months
Take educational standard to degree level	Investigate different methods of achieving this	1 month
	Book an appropriate course	3 months
	Get a degree or equivalent	5 years
Improve self-esteem	Find a mentor	3 months
	Read books about the subject	6 months

INSTANT TIP

As soon as you have a plan written down, you should start work on achieving your aims. It will be helpful to discuss your development plans with your mentor (or your boss or a friend if you have not yet found a suitable mentor) and make sure they are aware of the timescales so that they can prompt you into action and keep you on track.

Making a plan such as the one above will ensure that you focus on your priority areas for improvement. Putting a timescale on all the different aspects that you have decided you need to improve is essential so that your good intentions and actions so far do not go to waste. It is a good idea to put dates in your diary so that you feel committed to taking action and things are not allowed to drift, allowing your plans to take for ever to come to fruition. This will also help you to think about the sequence in which you think each action should happen so that you work to best effect. At the same time put a date in your diary (according to the timescales you have set for action) for a review of how much progress you have made. This will not only keep you on track but will also ensure that your plans are kept up to date and relevant to your current circumstances.

Of course, to be in a position to make a development plan you have to know where you are going. You also need to know yourself. There is plenty of advice in this book about identifying your values (Chapter 9), spotting gaps in your current skills (earlier in this chapter) and assessing your strengths and weaknesses (Chapter 5), so you will have to bring all this knowledge together in your development plan. This is something that will take a bit of time and should not be rushed. You will be at work for a long time so make sure that you give this the thought and time it deserves. Working out where you are going is rarely an easy task. Only if you have had a lifelong ambition – maybe a calling or a vocation – will you feel that the decision is made without a lot of soul-searching.

Many people start down a career path almost by accident and then spend the rest of their lives in a state of dissatisfaction. If you feel that your working life is boring or frustrating then this may have happened to you. The reason for this type of error is usually that we do not take control of our career choices – often until we feel it is too late. But none of the choices you make early on in your career is irreversible. So, if you're dissatisfied with your choices so far do not just accept your lot but make a start on real career planning now. Choosing the right career is a blend of finding your talents, working out what you actually like to do and playing to your strengths. It is certainly not necessary to stay in a job that you dislike but it will take effort to make a worthwhile change.

In the past few decades there has been a shift in career patterns. No longer do young people go into a career and expect to stay there for the rest of their working life. They are more likely to go through at least one or two changes and this can carry on until quite late in their working lives. Our working lives are becoming longer too, with an ageing population remaining fit to work into old age and also needing to work for longer as pension ages rise. People are even venturing into self-employment by starting new businesses well into their fifties and sixties. And of course, it's not just making the wrong choice that makes people need a career change. Personal circumstances change as we go through life and different things become important to us. It may be, for example, that while money was our main motivating factor when we took the job, we find that we don't need it as much as we thought or vice versa. Or it may be that the job itself changes with technological advances or changes in society. For example, how many shorthand typists are needed now with the advent of computers? Whatever the reason for the need for change, a considered approach will always work best.

Having worked out where you are with the help of this book, you will need to work out where you want to get to. Your values are especially important in this task as you will need to take into account what makes you happy – and what doesn't. As we said, you will also need to take careful note of what you can do and what you enjoy. Ask yourself questions such as:

- What do I enjoy doing in my current work role?
- What is my attitude to risk?
- What qualifications have I got – or could I get?
- What experience do I have?
- What comes naturally to me?
- What sort of organisation do I want to work in?
- Do I most like to be indoors or outdoors?

With the answers to these questions you should be equipped to define where you want to be. In the light of your answers consider your ideal job or field of work. If you find this difficult, get hold of a newspaper with lots of job advertisements in it. Now, ignoring your current qualifications and experience, which ones seem most appealing to you? If you are able to pinpoint a few jobs, this should guide you on your path. Note the requirements of these particular jobs. In broad terms, what are these employers looking for? This research will tell you not only about yourself and your likes, dislikes and attributes but also what types of job really appeal to you. These jobs might not be something that you are currently equipped for, but these choices can guide you towards where you should be heading.

Next you will need to figure out how you are going to get to where you want to go and that is where a development plan comes in. It will help to avoid unrealistic expectations if you consider your career as a journey. On any journey there may be false starts, stopovers, rewarding bits and some effort required. There is an ultimate destination but on a long journey, how you get there and what happens along the way will also be important. Your life's journey will include family commitments of some sort, money, work, leisure, community and retirement and all will have an influence on your career at different times.

At this point you should not view your qualifications, experience and skills as something that will hold you back or limit you to a specific career. Let your personal development plan help you to work out how you can broaden these things and allow you to achieve your aim. Very few people, if any, are only capable of one type of career so if you need a change, work out what you need to do to get there.

Assessing how development has helped your work performance

A comprehensive analysis of how the activities you have undertaken in order to develop have affected your performance will usually form part of your annual appraisal with your manager. It is always useful to discuss your development activities with your manager so if you do not have an appraisal or if it does not provide you with this opportunity then you must set up a meeting with your boss for this purpose. You need feedback on your efforts and on the benefits that they brought and it is your responsibility to manage this for yourself.

It is also useful to schedule regular reviews of your progress for yourself. You will want to see where your development activities have taken you so set aside some time to do this. If you have written down your personal development plan as described in the previous section you will have deadlines to meet for the various activities you have decided are necessary so these points are an ideal time to review the effect. If, for example, you have set yourself the goal of improving your educational standard to degree level as in the example above you would check after one month that you have the information you need and so on. Then you could go on to assess how taking that action has affected how you perform in your work role. It could have several effects, such as:

- Increased confidence – simply taking action is often sufficient to make you believe in yourself and your abilities.
- Increased motivation – even mundane tasks can be easier to carry out enthusiastically if you know you are making progress.
- Increased respect from others – if people, including your manager, know that you are trying to improve yourself they may view you in a different light.

Other changes and efforts that you make will have more direct effects on your work. It may be that you have acquired or improved a skill and you should monitor the effects of using that skill. Has it improved the results you obtain? Has it affected how you deal with others? Do you find it easier to do some aspects of your job – dealing with customers, for example? Make a note of all these effects so that you have something to remind you of what you have achieved. Finally, ask yourself if you have met your objectives and take this opportunity to set new objectives for the future.

SUMMARY

This chapter focused on possible gaps in your skills – first we looked at how to identify skills gaps, i.e. the gap between what your job requires and the actual skills that you possess. Understanding your skills, capabilities, experience and qualifications is the starting point, using your latest CV and expanding it to suit this purpose. A lot of questions need to be asked and answered to get a complete picture.

Having identified the gaps, we looked at ways to learn and develop including undertaking appropriate activities to

(Continued)

(Continued)

fill the gaps such as taking a course to learn another language. We examined the benefits to an organisation of a comprehensive training and development programme.

Next we discussed the help that mentors can provide in putting together a personal development plan and how to find a mentor. Mentors can provide career guidance, industry knowledge and can act as a sounding board.

Building a personal development plan was our next focus, with the emphasis on an organised approach with all actions to be taken written down and timescales set. We also looked at the questions about career choice and planning that can be invaluable in deciding where you want to be and how to get there.

We saw how undertaking development activities can help work performance by increasing your confidence and motivation and gaining respect from others in addition to filling specific skills gaps to help your career.

ACTION CHECKLIST

1. What skills gap would you say is most important to you currently?
2. How will you fill this gap? Have you set out actions with appropriate timescales for this?
3. Think carefully about your mentors. If you already have one (or more), consider their roles. If you do not currently have a mentor – think about who you could approach.
4. How far into the future does your current career development plan take you?
5. Consider your own choice of career. How did you get to where you are?

05

What do you need to do to develop yourself professionally?

Unless you are completely satisfied with your current position you will need to take steps to ensure that you progress in your career. Assessing your current role and your values will help you to begin to understand where you want to go and what needs to be done to get there and setting objectives will undoubtedly be a big step forward. All of these matters have been discussed in earlier chapters. What we need to look at now is just what you can do to make progress.

There are many activities that can be undertaken in terms of professional development and the important thing is to choose those that are particularly relevant to you and your situation. The areas that you should examine include:

● Qualifications – do you have the relevant qualifications for your current position and also to cover your future aspirations? If not, can you obtain them while working? Also, check that your employers are fully aware of your current qualifications.

- Experience – how much of what you have done in your working life and also in your personal life (perhaps you've done some voluntary work?) will be useful in your future career?
- Industry knowledge – are you up to date with developments in your industry?
- Contacts – have you developed a network of people who may be able to help you with your career development (and who you can help in return)? – see networking in Chapters 10 and 11

When undertaking professional development it is essential that you understand your own attributes so, in preparation for your development efforts, you should examine your own strengths and weaknesses. The next section will help you to do this.

Assessing your strengths and weaknesses

If you want to know yourself well you will need to know your own strengths and weaknesses and one of the most important ways of assessing strengths and weaknesses is to examine feedback from others. During our careers we will get feedback from all sorts of people in all sorts of ways and we consider it, use it to inform our behaviour where appropriate and then should store it up for future use. At various points in our careers it will be necessary to conduct an examination of our strengths and weaknesses in order to make the right move and to direct our careers in the best way to make the most of what we are good at and minimise the effect of our weak points. Without careful consideration of this feedback it is almost impossible to arrive at an objective assessment of our strengths and weaknesses. We sometimes fail to appreciate what is obvious to others.

There are many things about ourselves that we take for granted and maybe barely notice. These are the things that we find easy so we don't realise that this would be considered a valuable skill by those who don't possess it. It is only when someone else comments and says something like 'I could never do that' that we realise there may be a skill involved. A good example of this would be an ability to meet deadlines. Maybe you just do this automatically so it would be a strength for you or maybe you find this impossible to do so it would be classed as a weakness. Meeting deadlines is a collection of skills that would be valued by employers, such as planning and not procrastinating. If people often comment on how reliable you are or thank you for being on time with a project then you should count meeting deadlines as one of your strengths. But what if you have not been fortunate enough to have people commenting like this? How then will you identify your strengths? Try looking for the things in your working and personal life that you find easy to do or which just come naturally. This could include things like keeping your possessions in order, being on time, working steadily at a project, thinking logically, persuading others to help you, doing puzzles or even dancing – all of these are strengths that can be translated into things that employers would value in an employee. Conversely, your weaknesses are things that you find difficult and will, for example be the opposites of the strengths we mentioned. So always being late, finding it difficult to get help, having a short attention span when faced with a long project or being a poor dancer will be weaknesses.

Some of the things you will come up with may be things that do not, at first glance, appear to be something that most employers would be looking for. For example, your dancing skills or an ability to mend cars may not seem to make you the ideal employee (unless, of course, you plan to go into show business or be a car mechanic) but all skills, abilities, strengths and weakness have some relevance to employment. Let's look at a few examples:

Skill or attribute	Employment-friendly skill
Dancing	Good spatial skills
Mending cars	Problem solving
Creative crafts	Attention to detail
Cooking/entertaining	Presentation and coordination
Organised at home	Organised at work
Pessimism	Cautious approach
Optimism	Positive outlook
Doing puzzles	Analytical skills
Preparing family history	Research skills

These few examples should show you that there are lots of things that you take for granted but which are, in fact, strengths that make you more employable.

The idea when assessing your own strengths and weaknesses is to get to know yourself. If you look at your list of strengths you will see what you should be using to sell yourself to future employers and what should guide you in your choice of career. When you see your list of weaknesses you should see a list of things that you can work on. However, it is often quite difficult to really improve something that may be an intrinsic part of your personality so it may be best just to do what you can to minimise the effect it has on your life and, of course, not to mention it when applying for jobs in the future. You may also need to steer away from jobs that really need the strengths that you do not possess.

Gaining industry-specific knowledge

To be successful in any field you will need to know what is going on in your industry and to keep up to date constantly. If you do not have sufficient professional knowledge it will be difficult to keep up with your colleagues and it will be impossible for you to make fully-informed judgements in your work role and in your career. Even if you have extensive industry-specific knowledge, Continuing Professional Development (CPD) is something that you will often be required to do to maintain membership of professional bodies or your employer may require evidence of your efforts in this direction. It will certainly help you if you are looking for promotion or are applying for other jobs to further your career in the industry.

Developing your industry-specific knowledge is an essential task but can be time consuming. The purpose is to gain knowledge about your industry – specialist skills, trends, changes in the markets, relevant legislation and so on. There is a variety of ways in which you can do this including:

- Reading trade magazines and journals – your library will usually be a good source of information about these or ask your boss what they would recommend.
- Membership of relevant organisations – for example, professional bodies and trade associations.
- Research on the internet – competitors' websites, e-conferences, newsletters and so on.
- Training – this could be something that your employer suggests or self-funded online courses, for example.
- Finding a mentor – some organisations appoint a mentor or 'work buddy' for all new employees and this can be a very useful source of information and support.

- Conferences and exhibitions – not only will you get the specific information about the subject matter of the conference but it will also be an opportunity to talk with others in your industry.
- Networking events – more about this in Chapters 10 and 11 – will bring you into contact with others in your industry.

INSTANT TIP

If you are finding it difficult to further your industry-specific knowledge, ask the people around you at work and those you meet while you are networking what they think is the best source of information. Take advantage of what others have found.

A mixture of the above ways of keeping in touch and developing your knowledge of your industry is usually necessary but whatever you choose, you must develop a strategy for gaining this knowledge and keeping it up to date. Try not to leave this to chance but instead prepare a plan for yourself with time limits and targets as to how many types of information you will access and when.

Identifying your own learning style

The way we learn differs from person to person and it can be extremely useful, in the process of getting to know ourselves, to find out what will be an effective way for each individual to learn. This will enable optimum choices of learning activity to be made and to maximise chances of success. In addition, understanding your own learning style will enable you to plan to work on expanding the ways you can learn. As always, being aware of your own preferences and aptitudes will enable you to work around them and to maximise your learning opportunities. The key to success in this case is balance so that you do not concentrate too much on the way of learning that comes most naturally to you but develop your proficiency at using other methods.

Many ways of classifying learning styles have been tried and one of the most popular analyses of ways we learn centres on the senses we use to absorb information – the primary learning pathway. It is helpful to find our own learning style as this will ensure that we can look out for ways to learn that are appropriate for us and will make learning easier. The three learning styles that have been defined by psychologists working on Neuro-Linguistic Programming (NLP) projects are:

- Visual – this is where learning is sight based.
- Auditory – here the primary sense involved in learning is hearing.
- Kinaesthetic – this involves the sense of touch.

Try this quick quiz to discover your learning style. A lot of the clues to defining our learning style can be found in the things we say or how we tackle everyday tasks. Read these questions and decide which answer you would be most likely to give:

1. When checking the spelling of a word you would say:
   a That looks right.
   b That sounds right.
   c That feels right.
2. If you're trying to reassure someone that you understand what they are saying to you, you would say:
   a I can see what you're saying.
   b I hear what you're saying.
   c I feel that I understand what you're saying.

3. If you're buying a new piece of furniture or equipment for your home, what would influence your decision the most is:

   a How it looks.

   b The description given by the salesperson.

   c How it feels when you touch it.

4. What would be most useful to you if you were trying to assemble this new item of furniture or equipment?

   a A video of it being assembled.

   b Recorded instructions.

   c Trying to do it yourself.

5. What would help you to understand a mathematical problem?

   a Diagrams about how it can be solved.

   b Listening to someone's explanation of the solution.

   c A model of how it all fits together.

6. If you're trying to understand some new computer software, would you:

   a Read the manual that came with the software.

   b Ask a friend to come over and tell you how they use it.

   c Sit at the keyboard trying it out.

7. If you were choosing a book to read for pleasure, what would make you buy?

   a The look of the cover.

   b A friend talking about it and saying it was worth reading.

   c The book feeling heavy and glossy.

8. How are you most likely to give someone directions to your home?

   a Writing the directions down.

   b Telling them which roads to take.

   c Drawing them a map.

9. Think back to when you were at school. Which sort of lessons did you most enjoy?

   a Where the teachers drew diagrams or gave you a textbook.

   b Where the teacher told you about a subject.

   c Practical sessions.

10. Where would you be most likely to find a review of a film that makes you want to go to see it?
 a In a newspaper or magazine.
 b On the radio or from a friend telling you about it.
 c On the TV.

Now add up all your a's, b's and c's and check out the styles below.

- **If you got mostly a's**. Your learning style is visual. You learn best by seeing things. This might be by reading books or by watching television or educational videos. Anything you can do to enhance the visual impact of your learning materials will improve your learning experience and help you to remember what you have learned. For you, it will be a good idea to use different coloured highlighters and pencils when making any notes. You will know that you are a visual person if you say things like 'I see what you mean' or 'I can't see what the problem is.'

- **If you got mostly b's**. Your learning style is auditory and the most important sense that you use in learning is that of hearing. You will learn best by discussing things with others or listening to audio CDs and so on. Debates will help you tremendously and you could try explaining something that you find difficult to understand to someone else who has no knowledge of the subject. The things that you will say that will show that hearing is your primary learning pathway include 'Sounds OK to me' and 'I hear what you're saying.'

- **If you got mostly c's**. Your learning style is kinaesthetic. This means that the sense of touch is most important to you. Practical learning sessions will help you to retain information. The clues in the language you use that show that touch is most important to you include, for example, 'It feels good to me' or 'That touched a nerve.'

Although everyone will have a dominant sense that dictates their learning style, the very best approach for everyone is one that uses a combination of all senses to get the message across. Individuals will need to be aware of their own preferences and then play to their strengths as we have just detailed, while using materials that combine all the learning styles. Now that you know what is likely to work best for you, seek out the type of materials that suit you and will help you to retain the information you will need to be successful in your work role.

Do not, however, let knowing your learning style blind you to all the other ways to learn. If you concentrate exclusively on methods that you think will suit your way of learning you may miss something that would really help you. It is important, while knowing and catering for your learning style, to experiment with different methods of learning. We are all a mixture of styles and personality traits and these can change according to our mood and what's going on in our lives so we must remain open minded about learning methods.

Career development activities

All the previous sections in this chapter about professional development (and also the previous chapter about understanding your personal values) have been about understanding yourself – your strengths and weaknesses, your learning style and so on – but now we can get to the nitty gritty. We will look at some of the activities you can undertake to help you to develop your career.

One very important development activity that you should undertake is an assessment of where you are, how you got there and what you need to do to get where you want to go. Let's look at the steps in this process.

Decide where you are now

Assessing where you are now is a useful activity no matter where you are at in your career. You may be a senior manager or a junior employee with no responsibility for others so far, but you need to know and understand your starting point and what effect this will have on your future. In doing this, and developing an understanding of what your current role entails, you need to examine the following points:

- What is your job title?
- Does your job title describe your level of responsibility? If not, then describe it for yourself.
- What sort of organisation are you employed by? Is it large or small, which sector is it part of – public or private, charitable, non-profit – and what is its purpose?
- What are your responsibilities? For example, do you manage people, do you have a budget, do you have targets set for you?
- Are you settled in your job or do you view yourself as 'in transit'?
- How confident are you in your work role? Are you able to do it without too much effort or are there areas where you have a lot to learn?

In addition, you should consider feedback. This will include any appraisals you have had in your work role and any comments from colleagues and managers and other people who know you well. You can also get new feedback from colleagues, bosses past and present and career-minded friends by asking them three broad questions:

1. What do I do well?
2. What don't I do well?
3. What could I improve on?

All these views of what you have done so far in your career, your current performance and needs and what you are capable of achieving will be invaluable as you formulate your plans for the future.

Assess how you got there

This is a useful exercise in that it can show you what you've had to do to get to your current position, what sort of things you like and don't like, and what lessons you've learned along the way. Look at the progress you've made and consider what you had to do at each stage of your career to move forward. Sometimes these actions take place almost automatically and we do not fully consider the choices we have or take notice of what actions we have had to take. Did you, for example, have to gain extra qualifications or take on extra responsibility? Did you receive help from others – mentoring, for example? Look at how your capabilities have grown and developed and how you have dealt with extra duties or responsibility. Take particular note of the crossroads that you have arrived at from time to time. Can you identify any points in your career where you made a significant change – for example, moving up to management level or acquiring new knowledge or experience? How did you achieve this? What were your choices at the time? Were you comfortable in your progression or a little wary of major changes? How did you decide what move to make next – or does your career so far seem to have 'just happened'? Maybe this is your first real attempt to plan your career?

Looking back at previous jobs you have had and considering what you did and didn't like about them will also give you important clues about where you should be going. Not only will previous jobs be an indication of the experience you have but they will also point you towards success. Deciding what you did not like about some situations – perhaps you hated working in a large organisation, for example – is fairly easy but pinpointing just what you did like may be more difficult. Think carefully and you may come up with some examples of your likes such as when you were excited by someone making a success of a small business for themselves. Both of these examples would suggest that you may want to start a business of your own. It would be smaller and also may give you the opportunity to be an entrepreneur, which may be the aspect you liked about the small business. Also consider when you have been particularly happy. For example, were you happiest when you were at university or when you were doing voluntary work? This will show you where you should concentrate your efforts if you are looking for a change of direction in your career.

All of these things will help you to understand your career and yourself so that the next step – deciding where you want to get to in the future – can be taken in a more informed and considered manner.

Decide where you would like to be

This is an important step in your career development and you will need to spend some time on this, taking into account all that you have learned about yourself. Ask yourself questions such as:

- Just what do I want to achieve in my career?
- Why do I want this?
- What level do I want to reach?
- Do I want to stay in my current organisation or would I do better elsewhere?
- Do I want to manage?
- Do I want to take on training commitments?
- Do I want to change careers completely? Or to develop – and maybe progress – in my current choice of occupation?

- Is what I want from my career feasible?
- And finally, do I want to progress at all? Maybe you are happy just where you are.

It is important at this stage to take into account your personal values (see Chapter 9 for more details) and your current qualifications and experience. You should also consider your current and future commitments. This includes financial, family and social commitments. Some career decisions and aspirations require sacrifice in terms of time and money so your circumstances can affect what you need to do and what it is possible to do at this point in time. If there are things in your life that will stop you from achieving all you want to do in the long term – taking up a training course, for example, then there are two possibilities. First you can look for alternatives. Is the way you have ruled out the only way to achieve your aim? Could you, for example, take a course online in your spare time or could your employer help with time off for training rather than having to give up work to take a full-time course? There is often more than one way of achieving your objectives and the time spent considering all your options will not be wasted.

The second way that you can resolve a problem with your short-term plans is to make a longer-term plan. By doing this you may be able to see a time when your short-term difficulty – not being able to forgo your income in favour of a course of study, for example – will become less of a problem and you can plan what you need to do to get yourself in the right position. At this stage the important thing is to decide where you want to get to in your career and it is in the next stage that you will work out how to achieve your objectives.

Assess what you need to do to get there

This is the planning stage of your professional development plans. This is where you will set yourself targets and decide on the actions you need to take. Remember, if you set time limits on your goals you will be far more likely to achieve them.

Your first step should assess what will be necessary in terms of the skills you need to ensure the progression you want in your career. Look at this from two angles:

1. Do you need to strengthen existing skills?
2. Do you need to acquire new skills?

You can then make plans to bring your skills up to the standard you have decided is necessary. This may involve training courses or developing 'on the job'. If you are planning to approach your employer for help – perhaps funding for training or time off to do it – remember that your chances of getting help will be much greater if you can convince them of benefits to the business rather than simply presenting a case of how your training aspirations will benefit you. Will the training you are asking for mean you will be better equipped to gain new customers for your organisation, to complete change projects or to improve production processes? Whatever the planned improvement to your skills, relate this to something that you can deliver to your organisation and try to quantify this in terms of the benefits the organisation will gain. In addition, as always with any sort of planning, you should decide when you expect to achieve these improvements in your skills and when the organisation will realise the benefits. It is also essential that you decide how you will know the objective has been achieved. So, for example, if you are looking for funding for training that will give you project management skills, present a case to your employers that demonstrates the type of project you will be able to manage and when you expect to be up to this standard following your training. You should also, if possible, find out and mention the cost savings made with similar-sized projects in the past.

Although training is the obvious way of increasing your skills and achieving your development goals there are other ways that you can get to where you want to be. You may need to change your behaviour to effect some improvement. Perhaps you've had feedback in appraisals that have pointed to your lack of attention to detail, in which case you should have looked at why your work isn't always 100 per cent correct. You may conclude that you're rushing things and this would therefore be something that you should stop doing. To combat this tendency you could decide that you will plan more effectively in future and start a report or other task in plenty of time so that you are not rushing. Similarly, if feedback that you have received points to something that you are doing well then you could plan to do more of this. It may be that your manager has commented that you deal well with customers. This could point you in the direction of customer service or sales and this may be something that could increase in your work role if you choose to take it in that direction.

Apart from formal training opportunities, there are other ways in which your employer can help you to develop. They may be able, for instance, to arrange 'on the job' experiences for you. If you feel you would like to improve your customer-facing abilities, for example, they may be able to set up this sort of experience for you by letting you accompany a sales manager on visits to customers as an adviser in your own capacity. Meeting someone from a different department – the production or accounts department, for example – can be a helpful experience for customers and for the sales manager as well as for you. Your manager may also be able to think of projects that you can tackle – either in your own department or in another department – that will produce results for the organisation, perhaps by way of a report that you must complete at the end of the project, and also provide you with a learning experience tailored to your needs.

There are all sorts of skills and aptitudes that you can improve for yourself. The key thing is to appreciate what needs to be improved and then to figure out a way of improving it. It is best if this task is broken down into smaller objectives. So, for example, if your feedback and self-assessment has told you that you need to improve your presentation skills you could break this down into a number of elements of the skill that you can work on:

- building confidence
- finding out what makes a good presentation
- putting together a good presentation
- learning about an appropriate software program for preparing a presentation (e.g. PowerPoint©)
- practising speaking in public
- making a video of yourself making a presentation
- getting help in analysing what you are doing wrong
- planing a small presentation so that you can see if what you have been doing to improve your skills actually works.

Another excellent career development activity is networking. Chapters 10 and 11 will give you plenty of detail on how to do this and what benefit it can be to your career and work role but here we will just say that it can provide many benefits including sources of information, ways of increasing sales leads and obtaining mentoring from others in your industry.

The main thing to remember when taking steps to equip yourself for career improvements is to give this the attention it deserves. This is an activity to be taken seriously, so approach it in a business-like manner. Set goals, write them down, develop a written plan of action, break down large goals into a series of smaller tasks and set deadlines for your objectives. Write the dates in your diary and do the task on the day you have specified for yourself. You would do this for tasks you are carrying out for other people so why not do it for yourself? Your own aims and objectives are just as important.

If you have decided that you need to make big changes, perhaps moving to a different industry or organisation but find that you will have to wait some time for the right opportunity to come along you may feel trapped in your current situation. This is no reason not to take action. Try to create more opportunities where you are. These should be viewed as essential training and a way of acquiring new skills and may well lead to something worthwhile. For an example of how this might work, consider the case study below.

Case study

Simon, a young accountant in a medium-sized manufacturing company was bored in his job and had decided to move to another organisation. He was unclear exactly what else he could do but knew he did not want to be an accountant for the rest of his working life. He faced other problems in that he needed to maintain his salary level as he had a young family and the employment market was particularly difficult at that time so a move was out of the question in the short term.

Simon had noticed a problem with some of the accounts clerks who had been given new targets about contacting customers as part of a new customer service initiative. They were nervous and saw the new targets as being part of their employers' plans to try to make them into sales people. Simon had always enjoyed the customer contact part of his job, even though it had been limited, so he offered to set up a training programme to show them how to deal with customers by telephone. The course was a great success, the accounts clerks met their targets and Simon was given a sideways move into training. He enjoyed this job and built it up until he was made department head. When he next reviewed his career objectives he no longer saw a need to move to another organisation – he had achieved the change in career by a different means. The key thing is that when he had faced a stumbling block in his career plans, Simon did not stand still. He created his own job and found a solution to his problem.

When working on self-improvement, don't forget that you do not need to achieve everything at once. So long as you have a plan and an objective and are using that plan to work towards that objective then you will be going in the right direction. Improvement can be – indeed, often is – a gradual process.

What next?

When you have a plan of what you are aiming for in your professional life and have set goals to help you get there, it can be a good idea to leave it aside for a short while – perhaps a few days. During that time you will be subconsciously turning over the ideas in your mind and when you come back to your plan you may want to make some adjustments or it may be that you are convinced that this is the right path for you and your career. But don't leave it too long or you may find that you have lost some of your enthusiasm – or other things may push it out of your mind.

Most important though, is that you make a start. All the planning and assessing in the world will not help you to achieve your ambitions if you do not take action. Assess your plan and break it down further into small steps that you can take on the path towards your goal. So, for example, you may have decided that you need to gain a particular qualification to further your career. You can break this down into:

- Set a time when you will actually start studying.
- Research on the internet – who offers the right course for you?
- Can you go straight into the course to obtain the qualification you want or do you need to work your way up? Planning a viable route to obtaining the qualification you need is vital.

- Obtain prospectuses from the educational institutions that provide appropriate courses.
- Work out how you would make the time to do the course.
- Make your case to obtain backing from your employer.
- Approach your organisation for funding.
- Book the course.

All of these activities are things that pro-active employees will do for themselves but you should also be sure to do whatever you can to encourage your employer to develop a career development policy for employees.

Employers can be an enormous help in developing careers and forward-thinking ones realise that it is an important way to increase staff retention and to get the very best from their employees. They can do this in a number of ways:

- training opportunities – including cross-training, i.e. learning about other jobs in the organisation
- promoting from within
- establishing a mentoring programme.

Professional development is something that anyone with ambition should focus on. Taking responsibility for our own progress is essential if we are not to rely just on luck and circumstance. Knowing where you want to go and working out how to get there is the path to development and success in your career.

SUMMARY

In this chapter we looked at professional development and the actions you can undertake to make progress.

First we assessed strengths and weaknesses and considered how a variety of personal skills and attributes can indicate employment-friendly skills.

Next we examined ways to expand your industry-specific knowledge including reading trade magazines, joining professional organisations and attending conferences, exhibitions and networking meetings.

Knowing your own learning style was seen to be important in making activity choices and a questionnaire was used to check your dominant learning style – visual, auditory or kinaesthetic.

We then went through a process of deciding where you are now, assessing how you got there and deciding where you want to be, then assessing what you need to do to get there. We saw that this is a lengthy exercise, requiring lots of thought and then taking the appropriate action to improve.

ACTION CHECKLIST

1. Take one of your strengths and one of your weaknesses and assess the effect they have on your current work role.
2. Which of the ways to expand your industry-specific knowledge do you currently use and which, if any, do you think you can usefully add in to your development activities?
3. What is your learning style and how do you think it affects how you learn?
4. How do you think assessing how you got to where you are will improve your understanding of what you need to do to progress from here?
5. What actions do you think you need to take now to progress your professional development?

06

How can you make the best use of your time?

Making the best use of your time requires discipline and self-knowledge. You need to know the principles of good time management, have the discipline to apply them to the tasks in hand on a regular, ongoing basis and what is important to you in terms of your goals, objectives and job requirements. Making the best use of your time will produce many benefits, such as:

- improved performance
- more time for important projects
- meeting deadlines successfully
- gaining a reputation for efficiency
- less stress
- a better work/life balance.

To gain these benefits you will have to put in plenty of effort, take an organised approach and manage your time consistently. It is a major part of managing yourself.

Achieving a work/life balance

The different areas of our life – work, home and family, friends, spirituality, health and so on – are all important and all make calls on our time. The difficulty is in maintaining a balance between all these essential areas and not letting one area assume greater importance at the expense of other areas. Quite often, someone in the process of building a career or a business will spend disproportionate amounts of time on their working life while neglecting family responsibilities or to the detriment of their own health. It is widely acknowledged that a culture of working long hours while neglecting home life can lead to mental health issues.

Getting the balance right is essential if you are to make the most of your time and to give your very best performance in all areas of your life so you must find out whether or not your work/life balance is causing you problems. Try this quick questionnaire:

1. Do you often make promises that you don't keep? For example, 'Yes, I'll be home early tonight' or 'I'll phone you next week'?
2. Do you often feel too tired to go out?
3. Do you often feel ill?
4. Do some areas of your life command your entire attention for long periods while others are left out?
5. Do you have hobbies that you never get around to?
6. Do you ever feel guilty about areas of your life – for example, not having time to see friends or relatives?
7. Do you have to make excuses to friends, family or your boss about things you haven't done?
8. Do you feel that you never have enough time for you?
9. Do you often feel stressed?
10. Do you often feel irritable or anxious?

If you answered yes to even one of the above questions then it is likely that your life is not correctly balanced. Of course, the more yes responses you have the more your work/life balance needs attention. A severe lack of balance in your life can lead to problems including lack of performance in one or more areas and possible stress.

Achieving a work/life balance does not necessarily mean that you have to completely reorganise your life. It is more likely to be that minor changes here and there are all that is required and will be sufficient to put you back on track.

Case study

A manager of a large human resources department in the banking industry found that she was working very long hours, staying late at work on several evenings during the week and also taking work home. This cut into the time she spent with her family and gave her no time to herself. It made her feel guilty and also affected her performance at work as she always felt distracted. When she realised that she was neglecting her family and that the solution was in her own hands, she resolved to change. She cut back on her hours slightly by making sure that she finished on time at least twice a week. This gave her more time for her family but she still felt under pressure and as though she didn't have enough time to herself. She continually felt exhausted despite working shorter hours and realised the problem was that she never had any time to be alone. Both at work and at home she was dealing with other people's problems but could not find time for herself, so her health was suffering.

She made the decision to spend one evening a week on her own when she could do just as she liked. Sometimes she used this time to chat to friends on the phone, other times she watched TV or practised a bit of yoga and other times she simply sat and did nothing. This put her life back into balance and was something that she looked forward to every week. Within weeks of starting this 'me-time' she found that she felt energised and better able to cope with the stressful times at work.

Finding a balance is vital for our well-being and self-esteem but that balance will be different for each and every one of us. It is not a straightforward matter of allocating set proportions of time to all the areas of our life. And at different times of our lives it will be appropriate for us to spend more time and energy on one area than another. For example when we have a large, important project or deadline at work, it is likely that the majority of our time and efforts will be going on that and family or social life must take a back seat for a while. And when there's a new baby in the family or an elderly parent to care for then home life may need more attention than usual. The important thing is to maintain a balance that suits our circumstances for the majority of the time. It is also necessary to be honest with ourselves about the cause of any imbalance and appreciate that it is our life and only we can fix it. Many people make excuses for imbalances in their life, blaming a difficult boss, children with problems or a demanding partner, but it is up to us to deal with whatever life throws at us and to look after our own wellbeing.

If one area of your life is being neglected it can lead to stress with guilty feelings, strain and pressure all taking a toll on our health. There are three main elements to maintaining a balance in your life – control, relationships and perspective. Let's look at each of these.

Control

Feeling that we are in control of our lives is vital to our sense of wellbeing. If we feel that we have no choices and must do as other people want us to do then stress levels can quickly build. Having control of our day-to-day activities can ensure that we are able to choose to do things that move us towards our personal goals and objectives. This can give a feeling of achievement, which is important in motivating most people.

Relationships

Healthy, supportive relationships are important – at home, at work and socially. Feeling supported, appreciated and connected with the people with whom you have to work ensures that stress does not exceed bearable levels and problems can be dealt with. It is also vital to have a network of friends and family outside work that will provide a chance to relax.

Perspective

Blowing things out of proportion is a well-known symptom of depression so it is essential that we are able to view our situation in a realistic light, i.e. to keep things in perspective. It is easier to do this when we have clear goals and can see that what we are doing is contributing to those goals. This makes the problems we encounter and the hard work we have to cope with easier to deal with. Balancing this hard work and the more troublesome times against what we can achieve will give us this vital sense of perspective.

All of these three areas will need your close attention if you are to achieve and maintain an effective work/life balance. If there is a general problem in your workplace with, for example, a culture of long working hours and you are working in a highly pressurised environment, it can be useful to tackle the problems with the help of your colleagues. A concerted approach from a group of people in a workplace will obviously carry more weight and be far more likely to be listened to than just one person speaking up. A single employee may just be seen as someone with a gripe and then be ignored, so discuss the matter with your colleagues if appropriate and plan how you can deal with the problem. It is in any employer's interest to tackle problems of workplace stress as it can cause deterioration in performance, increased absenteeism, and sickness absence and an inability to retain good staff.

INSTANT TIP

Getting your work/life balance right is not something that you can do once and then ignore. It is something that you must review constantly to ensure you are still on track. Don't let problems creep up on you.

The next section discusses how you can deal with the stress that may be caused by work overload or by a lack of work/life balance.

Dealing with stress

Stress is becoming increasingly prevalent in the workplace and is causing problems not only for individuals but also for companies with affected staff. It also means that health providers are struggling to cope with the demands on them made by the huge numbers of people who are reporting work-related stress. Stress occurs when people are unable to cope with the pressures they are meeting in their everyday lives. Symptoms of stress are many and varied and can include irritability, fatigue, mood swings, digestive problems and skin problems. It is widely believed that today's increasingly fast pace of life is to blame for the increase in stress and it is indeed true that many people feel under intense pressure because of the way the world of work is run today and the way that communication is constant. Businesses are results-driven and highly pressurised and we have mobile phones and emails making constant demands on our time and interrupting us at all times. This can lead to stress, which in turn can lead to health problems such as depression, diabetes and heart disease. Of course, some pressure and stress in a work situation – and in life in general – is almost inevitable and can usually be a positive influence. However, problems occur when the pressures become too great.

There are three important things to do to make a start in dealing with stress, discussed below.

Recognise the problem

Friends and family can be a great help here as they will be able to tell you if you have not been quite your usual self. Perhaps they will have noticed irritability or a lack of focus and can give you helpful feedback on these traits. You may also notice signs in yourself such as reduced performance at work, a lack of interest in what is going on or making more mistakes and feeling tired. If you feel stressed, then you are indeed suffering from stress and it is up to you to discover the cause of this and deal with it.

Don't be afraid to change things

Even small changes such as getting away from work on time once or twice a week can make a difference to how you feel. Apart from the benefit of being able to spend time with family or friends, this will allow you to demonstrate to yourself that you are in control of your work rather than the other way round. An important way to make a change to your situation is to learn to say no. If you stop doing the things that you do only out of a sense of guilt or obligation, you will find that some of your stress disappears. If you do things that you do not really want to do not only will your time be taken up by the work entailed possibly resulting in overload, but you will also begin to feel irritated with others for asking you to do the task and with yourself for saying yes. If you say no to the things that you do not really want to do you will make time and space in your life to do the things that you enjoy and are rewarding for you.

Aim for a change of pace and focus

This change of pace and focus means taking your attention from work to something else. This could be in the form of exercise such as walking, swimming or a team sport, or a hobby such as playing the piano, reading or painting. The important thing is to change the pace of your day and to take the focus off the pressures that you are facing.

Although many people who do not work outside the home feel stress – even schoolchildren are reported to feel stressed by the demands placed on them in modern society – the majority of people who feel excessively stressed are in a work situation. There are several specific things you can do to reduce stress at work:

- Look after yourself – eat healthily, exercise regularly and get sufficient sleep.
- Know yourself – if you feel worried, work out why and deal with it. Make the necessary changes.
- Limit your commitments – if you know your limits and are assertive enough to say no when you know you are taking on too much, then you will keep your stress to reasonable levels.
- Manage your time – see later in this chapter for more details on how to manage your time effectively.
- Build a social life – this will help you to relax.
- Don't look for an argument – unnecessary conflict causes stress, so look for win-win situations where the outcome will benefit everyone.
- Accept what you can't change – there is no point wasting time trying to change the whole world and it is important to accept that some things just cannot be changed.
- Don't rely on artificial stimulants – alcohol, caffeine, drugs and nicotine will not solve your problems or even make them go away. Ultimately they will increase your stress levels.

- Do not let work encroach on your personal time via communications technology. Turn off your mobile phone and leave your laptop by the door when you get home.
- Take time out to relax – it is not a waste of time to do this as you will work harder after a break.

The important thing is to deal with stress before it becomes a serious health issue. If you have tried the above suggestions and still feel anxious, it would be advisable to see your GP. You should also discuss the issue with your employers as they have a duty to ensure the health and safety of their employees.

Where does your time go?

If you know that you need to make better use of your time your first task must be to find out exactly where your time goes. You need to know how much time is spent on essential tasks, how much on time-wasters (see the section later in this chapter), how much on things you could delegate and how much on yourself and the things that will keep life outside work going. After all, if you don't know just where your time is being used then how will you be able to use it better? Tracking your activities is the first step to managing the use of your time.

So, how do you analyse your use of time? The easiest way is to keep a time log over a period of a week. Write down everything you do – including sleeping, eating, watching TV, travelling, jobs at home as well as everything, no matter how trivial, you do in the course of your job. Note down every interruption, every meeting and phone call as well as time spent working on major projects and planning time. At the end of the week, group all similar activities together so that you know how much time, over a week, you spend on things such as writing, phone calls, research, checking emails and meetings as well as things you do at home. This can all seem like a difficult and unimportant task but it will be well worth the effort. With a list that tells you how many hours you spent on the phone or attending meetings, for example, you will be able to see where time can be saved. Obviously, some things will be things that you cannot cut down on such as eating (unless, of course, you're having long lunches during your working day!) or travelling (unless you could arrange to work at home one or two days per week) but most of the things you do during your working day can be examined to see if there is a more efficient way of achieving the same results without spending so much time.

Next you must deal with what you have found out about how you spend your time. The section below on prioritising your objectives will help you when you have arrived at a list of things that you must do. But first you can eliminate many of the things that you currently do. Many unimportant things become habit – that cup of coffee before you start work or the chat with the receptionist every morning as you arrive for example – and you can eliminate them without too much damage and will then save appreciable amounts of time taken over a week or month. Alternatively, you can simply change some of these unnecessary uses of your time by reducing or limiting them, for example. You could also decide to rearrange some tasks. This works particularly well with phone calls or checking emails.

You can group all the same tasks together into perhaps one or two periods per day. In this way, you will save transition time – the time spent moving from one activity to another, including the time lost by interruptions in concentration. If you are writing a report and are continually interrupted by telephone calls then the two tasks together will take far longer than if you were to write the report without interruptions and then deal with the phone calls in a separate session.

We have, of course, concentrated here on how you spend your time during your working life but a similar approach to how you spend your time outside work can produce good results. In both cases you will probably be surprised by how much time you spend on relatively unimportant matters such as exchanging gossip at work, or on reading magazines or watching television, but do remember that some relaxation is essential and that achieving and maintaining a work/life balance is just as important as getting everything done in the shortest possible time. It cannot be put better than the old adage – 'work smarter, not harder'.

INSTANT TIP

Managing your use of time is about changing your behaviour. So, if you identify that you spend a lot of time on one particular activity at work that is not essential to meeting your goals then you need to reduce the amount of time spent on it – no matter whether you enjoy that activity or not.

Prioritising tasks

One of the most important aspects of managing your time effectively is making sure that you do the things that matter most first. Deciding what these things are will involve rating them according to whether they are important and then deciding the urgency with which they need to be done. A useful tool in reaching this sort of decision is the 'urgent/important rule'. To do this you must rate each task on your to-do list that needs prioritising according to how urgent and/or important it is.

So, using the urgent/important rule, the list of tasks will be dealt with as follows:

- If it is decided that something is urgent and important you need to do it immediately.

- If it is urgent but not important you can choose to delegate it or plan to do it yourself later.
- If a task is important but not urgent it can be planned into future activities.
- If it is decided that a task is neither important nor urgent then it doesn't need to be done.

At this point you may be asking yourself 'But how do I know if something is important?' (urgency will usually be more obvious). The simple answer to this is to ask yourself two more questions – 'Does it contribute in some way to my goals and objectives?' and 'What will be the consequences of not doing this task?' The more it will contribute to achieving your goals and objectives, and the worse the consequences of not doing it, the higher up the list of priorities it should be – it is more important to you.

As always, even your list of priorities will benefit from regular review. So, if you don't get everything on your list completed in one day, for example, go through the priority exercise again, adding tasks and deleting them as necessary according to changes that you will have to react to. At first, this may seem to take up valuable time but if done regularly it will become second nature and will help to ensure that everything that really matters gets done. You may well find after some time that there are tasks that fall by the wayside and never make it on to your to-do list as they are not important enough. Either these things do not need doing or you will delegate them to someone else.

If you tackle tasks according to the urgent/important rule you will find that you will be unlikely to ignore something that will have long-lasting consequences if not done and you will be spending time on the things that really matter.

INSTANT TIP

It's a good idea to have a prioritising session at the start of each working day. Go through your to-do list and decide if everything on it is urgent and/or important – if it's neither, cross it off the list! Next decide the approximate order for carrying out your remaining tasks. Just 10–20 minutes spent doing this each day will increase your effectiveness out of all proportion to the time and effort spent.

Setting deadlines

Deadlines, whether imposed on you by others or set by you for your own purposes, are important. They can help to focus the mind on a task, especially if you are the sort of person to leave starting work on a project until the very last minute so that if there is no deadline you may never get the job done. Many people put off starting a task simply because they feel uncomfortable with it or are unsure about how to go about it so deadlines are a good way to make you get out of your comfort zone. They should be viewed as a way to get yourself organised and are certainly an essential tool in managing yourself.

There are some common mistakes that people make when setting deadlines and avoiding these mistakes means your deadlines are more likely to be met and your performance correspondingly improved. Let's look at these and how to avoid them.

Long deadlines

Don't make the deadline too far away as this can lead to a lack of motivation. You will be most likely to take action about a deadline that is very close. If you have a long-term project, go ahead and set a finishing time for the project as a deadline but also set interim deadlines – milestones along the way – as these will carry you through to the end.

Unwritten deadlines

All objectives – and this includes deadlines that you set for yourself or are set for you – are far more effective when they are written down and acknowledged. If your deadline is, in fact, merely an idea in your head about when you would like to finish a task then it is less likely to be met than a properly formulated, considered deadline that is put into writing – even if this is just a note in your diary.

Impossible deadlines

If you know when you are setting the deadline – or when the deadline is set for you – that it is not possible to meet it then it will not motivate you and your performance is likely to be worse than if a realistic deadline to aim at was set.

Insufficient information

It is essential that you research a project or task thoroughly before setting a deadline. If you do not have the relevant information then the deadline will be meaningless.

Setting deadlines is a task closely allied to goal setting. So, when you have a goal you should almost always set a deadline for it. The following steps will help in setting deadlines:

1. Write down your goal then evaluate all the aspects of that goal that will help you to reach a realistic deadline.
2. Then consider all the resources you will need to reach your goal. For example, take into account how much time you will be able to dedicate to it, who else might have to be involved, any special knowledge you will have to acquire and research that will need to be done.
3. Next consider what the consequences are of not completing the task on time.
4. You will then be in a position to set a deadline using your diary to plan in 'mini-goals' for you to accomplish and to work out when, given the time you are able to allocate to it, your goal will be met. Mark it clearly in your diary – as we said, a written objective is always taken more seriously than one that is just an idea.

If you can develop a reputation for meeting deadlines then you are far more likely to be viewed as a valuable member of staff and to get a promotion when the time is right. Your performance will undoubtedly be improved by properly set deadlines.

INSTANT TIP

As an extra incentive to meet deadlines, give yourself a small reward when you meet a major deadline. This could be something simple such as a day off or a meal out. Having something that marks the end of a piece of work will help you to work towards it.

Dealing with time-wasters

In any work situation there will be a number of time-wasters that must be dealt with if you are to make the most of your most limited resource – time.

The telephone

Most people will answer a ringing telephone even when they are concentrating hard on something else. The telephone seems to command everyone. And of course these days we are always contactable because of mobiles, so the problem is even worse than it used to be. The main way to take control of the telephone is to designate certain times of day to make or to receive calls. You should also control who you speak to and why.

INSTANT TIP

Try keeping a log of phone calls for just one day. Keep separate logs of incoming calls and of those you make. Use this to decide where time is wasted.

Emails

These can be time-wasters if you are constantly checking them and they are allowed to interrupt other activities because you feel you have to reply straight away. Again, the solution is to schedule times for dealing with them. Limit the number of times you check for emails to, say, once at the start of the day, again at lunchtime and then late afternoon. When you open an email you should decide what to do with it there and then – and do it. You can reply, forward it to someone else, file it or delete it.

Visitors

If visitors, customers for example, are scheduled then they should not cause too much of a problem, especially if you can control the length of the meeting, perhaps by mentioning another commitment that you have directly after the meeting. The visitors who can become a problem are the casual visitors who call into your office unannounced or the ones who stay for a chat even after their business has been concluded. To ensure that this type of visitor does not waste your time at work requires a strict approach and will also need to take account of the policies of the organisation. Some businesses are happy for employees to have a 'closed door', not accepting interruptions during certain times of the day, while others will maintain that people should always be available. If visitors and phone calls become a real problem in your organisation, you will have to make a case for each member of staff having control over their own availability.

Paperwork

Dealing with and storing too much paperwork causes us to work less efficiently so we all need systems in place to ensure that we keep it under control. We should aim to handle each piece of paper that we send or receive just once. Often, we will read a letter when we receive it, put it down for a day or two, pick it up, read it again to remind ourselves of what it contains, then take the action needed. We then file it at a later date. So, we've handled it three times or more (maybe we shifted it about our desk in various piles before we decided what to do with it). It would be far more efficient to receive it, read it, decide what action to take – deal with it, pass it on, file it or throw it away – in just one hit.

INSTANT TIP

One way of controlling paperwork is to stop some of it before it reaches you. This can be done by getting your name taken off junk mail lists and signing up to the Mailing Preference Service – visit www.mpsonline.org.uk or call 0845 7034599.

Meetings

Meetings, if properly run, can achieve a lot, but they can also be one of the worst time-wasters in an organisation. Many meetings are far too long, sloppily run and do not achieve their objectives, if, indeed, any objectives were set for them. Also, the matters dealt with in meetings can often be dealt with more effectively by other means.

So, how can you make sure that meetings do not waste your time? This can be a three-pronged approach – attend fewer meetings, try to achieve the objectives without actually holding a meeting and also make sure they are run more productively. Let's look at these one by one in more detail. First, you can attend fewer meetings simply by being unavailable. To ensure that you are still 'kept in the loop' you could send a member of your staff in your place, if appropriate, or ask for a copy of the minutes, or to be kept informed by the chairperson or secretary, perhaps by giving you a quick summary of what went on in the meeting. You could also submit your comments and action points in writing prior to the meeting.

Second, suggest that your organisation holds fewer meetings by using teleconferencing or video conferencing. Meetings held in this way must be organised in a similar way to face-to-face meetings. They will need a chairperson and secretary, the usual documentation such as an agenda and minutes, and everyone should be aware that there is still a need to prepare for them as they should for any other meeting. Time savings can be made as you don't have to travel to meetings and they generally take less time.

The third way of saving time spent on meetings is by making sure that meetings are run correctly. This can be done by setting objectives for every meeting and by the chair person keeping a careful track of time, not allowing anyone to veer off the subject. Of course, you may not be in a position to affect the number of meetings held in other departments or to chair meetings but you can always make suggestions as to alternative meeting methods, attend fewer meetings yourself and, as an attendee, keep to the point and be clear about what each meeting is to achieve.

Procrastination

Many people frequently put things off but this only makes the task harder to tackle and wastes time as it will take longer to do if left for too long. So, why do we do it? The main reason for procrastination is fear – usually a fear of failure – and the only way to conquer this fear is to get on and do it. When you have tackled something, even if you may not have done it perfectly, then the fear of the task will have gone. If you are daunted by the size of a task, then the best way to tackle it is to break it down into more manageable chunks. For example, writing a report could be broken down into a number of stages including research, planning, outlining and finally, writing. If all you have planned to do is research some details, then it will be easier to take on the task. Of course, the writing could be broken down even further into the different sections of the report. In this way, the task will not seem quite so daunting.

'Fire fighting'

If you find that you are constantly managing in a crisis then you are wasting time. Doing things right first time is far more productive and a much better use of your time than putting right what has gone wrong.

Not saying 'No'

The skill of being able to say 'No' to requests that do not fall in with your own priorities and will not move you closer to your own goals is a really useful time management skill and one which you should make every extra effort to develop. If you are constantly agreeing to requests for help then you will often be furthering someone else's aims rather than your own. You can learn to say no to requests politely but in a way that leaves people in no doubt that you are unable to help them. Try 'No, I'm sorry, I'm too busy.'

The main defence in dealing with time-wasters is to identify the ones that waste the most time in your working life. We all have different ways of wasting time – some are even enjoyable! You may find it pleasant to chat on the phone to business colleagues but unless you are achieving something that will take you towards your objectives or you have decided that this is a relaxation period, then it is a waste of your time. Of course, some pleasantries are necessary in your working life and will help to smooth your path but control must be exercised if this is a problem area for you. On the other hand, your particular way of wasting time may be in the meetings you hold with your staff. If you regularly arrive early for them and spend the spare minutes chatting, do not have a specific objective for the meeting, nor keep a strict check on the time it takes, then this is a problem area for you and must be changed to use your time more effectively. The best way to identify your particular time-wasters is to analyse how you use your time as detailed in the section earlier in this chapter.

When you know what wastes your time you will be able to deal with the problem. Too many interruptions from telephone calls, for example, can be dealt with by using an answering machine or voicemail. This will enable you to reply to phone calls when it's convenient and to decide who you speak to and when. This, like most ways of dealing with time wasters, requires discipline. If all your calls are stored rather than answered as and when they arrive, in order for you to avoid interruptions you will have to plan some time into your day for answering the calls and dealing with the actions that become necessary. Similarly, plenty of discipline will be required to reduce the number of interruptions you get from casual callers. It can be tempting to stop work if someone calls in to your office when you are doing a difficult or disliked piece of work but if you have a strategy in place and apply your rules with discipline then your visitors will undoubtedly be able to waste less of your time. You could, for example, make it clear that you will not accept visitors in the mornings or on certain days of the week, or tell all callers (except, perhaps, your boss) that you are busy and will get back to them later. Alternatively, simply shut your door, creating a barrier that will deter many callers. Whatever your most problematical time-wasters are and whatever strategy you use, you must apply the solution with discipline and get the time-wasters out of your life.

SUMMARY

In this chapter we concentrated on time management and on maintaining a work/life balance. We saw that there are three main aspects of maintaining balance – taking control, having healthy, supportive relationships and keeping a sense of perspective.

The result of a lack of balance is often stress, which can become a serious health issue. We looked at what can be done to deal with stress including recognising the problem, not being afraid to change things and aiming for a change of pace and focus. We also noted a variety of specific things you can try.

Next we moved on to time management. A starting point is analysing exactly where your time goes so that you can eliminate what is unnecessary. The next step is to prioritise tasks using the urgent/important rule, ensuring that the tasks that contribute to your goals and objectives are given priority.

Next we looked at how deadlines can help and at the mistakes to avoid when setting them including setting deadlines that are too far away, impossible to attain or set using insufficient information.

Another aspect of time management is dealing with time-wasters and interruptions such as the telephone, emails, meetings, visitors to your workplace, procrastination, crises and not being able to say no.

ACTION CHECKLIST

1. Do you consider yourself to have a good work/life balance? If not, what do you feel you can do to improve it?
2. What do you consider to be the most stressful aspect of your working life – and what can you do to deal with it?
3. Note exactly how you use your time for just one day. Next, select one type of activity and assess how you can reduce the amount of time you spend on that activity.
4. Which of your current deadlines do you feel is going to be the most difficult to meet and why?
5. What is your biggest time-waster at work – and what steps have you taken to deal with it?

07

How does your work role fit into your organisation?

Fully understanding how your work role fits into the organisation you work for will allow you to see how your contribution affects the organisation. You will also be able to evaluate the effect of any improvements you make. While you may want to improve your qualifications, for example, for your own purposes such as to broaden your education or to obtain a better job in the future, anything new that you learn and any advances in your academic achievements will simultaneously affect the organisation. You should be aware of this and make sure that you keep your employers informed about any improvements so that they can, perhaps, reward you accordingly or include you in plans for the future. Another reason for being aware of the impact improvements can have on the organisation is that any actions you take to improve may be dictated by this impact. So, for example, if you become aware that you are lacking a skill that would help you in your current work role, then you will be able to take steps to acquire that skill.

Seeing how your work role fits into the organisation obviously requires a certain level of understanding of the organisation and your first step must be to make sure that you have this. If you do not feel that you already possess sufficient information about the organisation, how it works and the roles that are involved, you will need to get hold of a diagram of the roles that currently exist and see where your position fits into this. This will be a starting point for understanding the impact your work can have on others in the organisation, its results and on the organisation itself. Note, for example, how the different departments are set up. Is the organisation split into departments for different functions or by product group? How many levels of management are there? And, most importantly, where do you fit in? Who does your manager report to? Can you see a clear progression for yourself in the future? It can also be useful to think about the emphasis that your organisation places on the different work areas. For example, are the financial people in the organisation the ones who would be considered to be 'running the show' or is the organisation 'product led'?

Next you will need to think about your level of responsibility and about how you deal with other departments. Is your role important to others in the organisation? If so, to whom, and why? Consider what impact your work has on the aims and objectives of other people, both in your department and in other departments. Check out your job description for mentions of other departments. Do you have to supply information on a regular basis to other departments? Do others have to supply you with data or is there something that they do that affects when or how you can do parts of your job? All of these things will give you clear indications of where your work role fits in.

It is this level of understanding and giving plenty of thought to your work role that will lead to improvements in your performance and you will be able to manage yourself and your career much more effectively.

Evaluating your current work role

A thorough understanding of exactly what you do on a day-to-day basis and what skills you need to perform your duties is essential if you are to manage yourself successfully. The effort you will have to put in to do this evaluation could be repaid in two ways:

1. The understanding of your work role will enable you to carry out your duties better.
2. You will make it easier to produce a CV that will help you to progress in your career.

There are two aspects of your work role that you will need to understand. There is a theoretical view of what your job entails and also an actual view. The theoretical description of your job will be found in documents such as a job description and/or a person specification for the job and you should obtain copies of these if you do not already have them. (Maybe you've used them for exercises such as those described earlier?) The job description should detail the objectives of the job plus the responsibilities it entails and what tasks are to be undertaken. The person specification, on the other hand, will show you the kind of person that the organisation believes is required to do the job. This will detail the knowledge, qualifications and previous experience needed and will outline the abilities required.

The more practical view of your job will be found in your day-to-day tasks, the requirements placed on you by your manager and by other departments, customers and so on. A useful task at this point is to complete a log of how you actually spend your time. Set up a schedule, split into 15-minute slots of time. On this you can record, briefly but accurately, just what you do for a period of at least a week. Then list your tasks in broad categories such as planning, dealing with staff, customer contact and so on, and add up the amount of time you spend on each category. If, when you have completed this for one week, you feel there are other things that you spend your time on (a lot of this will depend on the level of your job as the more senior you are it is likely that there will be more long-term requirements of your work role) then add these to the list. You may, for example have monthly staff communication meetings that may not appear on a list of tasks completed in one week. With this information about how you actually spend your time to hand you should be able to see what is important in your work role.

These two viewpoints – what the organisation requires and what you actually do – should, of course, be broadly similar. However, if there are major discrepancies then you will need to delve deeper and ask yourself if either view is wrong – the written material giving the theoretical view or your own view of what you are doing. A chat with your manager should resolve this issue for you and deepen your understanding of your work role.

Taking into account both the theoretical and actual views of what your job entails, you now need to compile a list of the competencies, skills and knowledge required to carry out your duties. Give this plenty of consideration as this must include attributes such as analytical skills as well as the more obvious ones such as knowledge of basic facts or about your organisation. Consider how your work role affects the organisation as a whole. What would be the effect of your work role being removed? Which departments would be affected and how? Would the organisation's performance deteriorate, and in what way?

When you have got all this information together you will be able to see just what is involved in your work role and it will be useful, if you can, to discuss this in detail with your line manager. In a general discussion based on your list they will be able to give you more information about just what your role involves and it will be a useful opportunity for you to ensure that your understanding of the role is the same as your manager's.

Knowing your organisation

Knowing your organisation and your own role in it will help you to improve and develop. It can be fairly easy to do a job routinely, following instructions and not going further than what is asked of you, but ultimately this type of day-to-day performance will be unsatisfying and will not gain you promotion or assist in your own personal development.

So, if you feel you need to learn more about your organisation, what can you do? First, it could be useful to make this need known to your manager. They should be able to point you in the right direction and possibly may be able to give you lots of advice and information. Discussing your desire to know more will also flag up your interest. Second, you can check out all sorts of information that is readily available, including:

- Your organisation's website – here you may find details of its history, management, products, aims and mission statement and so on.
- Your organisation's intranet – many organisations now supply information to employees using an online system. This could include details of current projects, new products, feedback from customers, positions available and any changes going on in the workplace.
- Check if there is an induction course for new employees – these often set out the basics about an organisation. If this was introduced after your arrival at the company you may be able to take part in the next course or to be supplied with the course notes.
- Marketing literature produced by your organisation – this may include product specifications, sales leaflets, price lists and so on.
- Your colleagues – workers in both your own department and in other areas of the organisation will, no doubt, have lots of information about the organisation.

- Your organisation's newsletter – if there is one. This may be aimed at staff, in which case it may include new developments, social events, articles about members of staff, or it may be aimed more at customers, in which case it will probably include articles about the organisation's products and so on.
- Local newspapers – look out for articles about your organisation and what it may be doing in the community, job advertisements, awards the organisation or its staff may have won, and new plans in the pipeline.
- Trade press – get hold of copies of magazines that are geared towards your industry as they may contain articles about your organisation. Senior managers often get sent these magazines, so ask around.

INSTANT TIP

If you read a few trade magazines relevant to your industry and find that your organisation is not featured at all, ask why not. Approach the marketing department and find out if articles are submitted – perhaps you could write one? It is never a bad career move to be seen as an expert in any area.

A third option is to approach either your manager or the human resources department with a view to getting some cross-training i.e. training in other people's jobs, or perhaps you could spend some time in other departments to further your understanding of the organisation. Most organisations are amenable to this sort of request as it not only shows enthusiasm but also allows them to help staff development and the organisation may benefit if job or department changes occur in the future. Only very short-sighted organisations would try to stop you developing yourself and your knowledge.

There is no doubt that increasing your knowledge of the organisation in which you work will pay dividends for both you as the employee and for your employer. It will not only help you in your day-to-day work role but will also help you to see how you can progress in the future.

Reviewing your contribution

It is always a good idea to be fully aware of just what you are contributing to your organisation. If you want to progress in your career, either in your current organisation or at others in the future, you will need to be able to show proof of what you have achieved and to be able to cite examples. Keep details of all targets and objectives that you are given together with how you have performed against those targets. Also, keep any complimentary letters and so on that you may have received. You should be looking for details such as:

- sales figures and targets
- savings you have made for your organisation
- bonus payments received along with statements showing how you have performed against targets
- letters from customers thanking you
- details of any major changes that you have brought about
- major customers that you have dealt with
- commendations from your employers
- major projects you have taken part in
- suggestions you have made that have been adopted.

To review your contribution to the organisation you work for you should start with your job description. What are you meant to be doing? What is the purpose of your job? Then, with the help of your manager if possible, review how you are performing against the job's requirements. You need to look in detail at the results you have produced and what you have achieved. Have you carried out your work as expected or do you need to learn and develop in order to contribute more? Are you contributing less or more than you should be to the organisation? Again, your manager's input into this review process will be invaluable.

Make sure that you do not ignore less tangible contributions such as being part of a successful, cohesive team and facilitating other people's work. Your contribution is what you put into the organisation and you must be aware that there are lots of ways to contribute, so don't overlook any of them. The more you understand about the organisation, your role in it and exactly what you are contributing, the better you will be able to manage yourself and your career. There is great satisfaction to be gained from contributing properly to your organisation.

Where will you be in the future?

With a deeper understanding of your current situation as a result of your information collation about your role, you will be in a position to review your future prospects. Do you see yourself progressing steadily in your current organisation or moving to another organisation to realise advancement in your career? Or perhaps you have decided on a career change and will be taking up learning opportunities in another field or starting at the bottom in a completely different career. Even if you have come to the conclusion that you are happy where you are, you will still need to be aware that things will probably change in your organisation or in the requirements of your work role in the future and some preparation for this eventuality must be made. The world of work will never let you simply stand still. Making your own changes and improvements is far preferable to having changes forced on you when you are not prepared. Whatever you have decided, you will make better progress if you set some goals for yourself and formulate a plan that will keep you focused and on track.

A first step if you are hoping to progress your career with your current organisation (apart from getting the information together and thinking about your role and your attributes) is usually to discuss your prospects with your manager. This could take the form of a regular appraisal so that you will know where you are going and what you need to do to get there, or it could be that you need to make arrangements for a formal discussion with your manager outside of the appraisal schedule. Either way, a frank discussion about your prospects with your boss is always illuminating. Make sure that you are prepared for such a discussion by collating information about your role and your achievements as detailed above.

Alternatively, if you feel that you will have better career prospects if you move from organisation to organisation, you will need to develop your knowledge of the job market and possibly the training that you will need to undertake to achieve your ambitions. If you are looking to change jobs then networking will become especially important to you – more about this in Chapters 10 and 11 – and this will provide you with knowledge about things outside your current organisation. Networking may also help you to find another job. In this case you need to give consideration to arming yourself with all you need to change jobs. This may include:

- a newly updated CV complete with relevant details about experience and qualifications
- details of the work you have been doing
- a description of the contribution you have made to your current organisation
- details of any special projects you have taken part in
- consideration of your values and what you are looking for in a new organisation.

However, even if you do decide to move to another organisation, don't neglect your current job requirements. It is usually the case that what you are doing now and how it is judged will affect your future. For this reason you should be continually reviewing and updating your skills and how you use them in your current job. Focusing on the future at the expense of the present will not necessarily make everything happen – remember, you will need references from your current employer and whatever you can achieve may enhance your CV. Also, remember that things are constantly changing in business and you need to be alert to opportunities in your current organisation as well as outside it.

Finally, in this section, note that personal management and career development is not something that is done occasionally, it is a continuous process.

SUMMARY

This chapter concentrated on how you and your role fit into your organisation. We started by evaluating what you do on a day-to-day basis by using your job description, your person specification and, of course, your own experience in the role.

We then looked at how you can find out more about your organisation using a variety of sources such as its website, intranet, marketing literature, newsletters, colleagues and your manager.

Next we saw how your role and your performance in it contribute to the organisation and the importance of keeping details of your achievements for future use. As we saw, a thorough understanding of your current role and organisation can help in a review of your future prospects – either in your current organisation or if you decide on a change.

ACTION CHECKLIST

1. Consider how your job description matches up with what you do day-to-day. Are there things you do that are not mentioned or things you should be doing but don't?

2. If you found things that you do not do but which are mentioned in your job description, why is this? Is this a situation that you should remedy?

3. If you haven't already done so, read your organisation's website in detail. Read every bit – even the 'Contact us' page and so on, and consider if the information given is both correct and comprehensive. Is there anything there of which you were unaware?

4. Review your contribution to the organisation and decide what has been your greatest achievement.

5. Consider how your performance and experience in your current work role will affect your future work situation.

08

How can you obtain, and then use, useful feedback?

Constructive feedback can be a very useful tool in improving performance so, in managing yourself, obtaining and dealing with feedback is an essential skill. It can:

- reinforce productive behaviour
- eliminate behaviour that is hampering an individual's performance
- enhance performance.

So, how do you obtain useful feedback? The short answer to this question is 'Ask for it'. But how do you ask for feedback that will be useful and how will you make use of it when you've got it?

Your first task will be to pinpoint the people who will be able to give you constructive and useful feedback about your work – more about this in the next section.

Next, you must evaluate what you have been told and then use it to improve your performance – this is also covered in this chapter.

The important thing is to be as objective as you can be about any feedback that you receive and this can be difficult. If you see the feedback as critical then you must try not to react defensively as this will not improve anything. Instead, see it as something that may be able to help you. You must then take action by dealing with the feedback, giving it full consideration and doing whatever is necessary to resolve any issues that have been raised. Feedback without corresponding action is useless.

Who is in a position to give you objective feedback on your work role?

Your main sources of feedback on how you are performing at work will obviously be people at work – your manager, the HR department and your colleagues. Depending on the nature of the feedback you require, you can ask, or will be given without asking, feedback that you should use constructively. It may be that you require feedback on your general performance and in this case the best person to ask will usually be your immediate boss. If you require feedback on how a particular task is going then asking someone working alongside you on the same task might be more appropriate and if you are a manager and want to evaluate and improve your performance as a manager then one of your most important sources of feedback will be the people who report to you.

A good opportunity for feedback is your regular appraisal with your boss. This will usually take place annually but there may also be a system in place for your performance to be reviewed more regularly. It will be useful here to consider just what you should expect to gain from an appraisal. It is an important part of your personal development activities and you should prepare carefully to ensure you get the greatest benefit from the process. Consider the following gains you may make from a routine, annual appraisal:

- a review of your past performance – this is the minimum you should expect: have you met your goals and objectives? And if not, why not?
- feedback from your manager
- coaching from your manager as you discuss tasks you have undertaken in the previous year
- an assessment of your team's performance
- setting goals and objectives for your work role in the next year
- an identification of your development needs in relation to your job
- a future development plan
- an assessment of your future in the organisation
- a view on your long-term career progression
- tasks delegated by your manager so that you can use them as development opportunities.

As you can see, the appraisal process is a major opportunity for you not only to obtain valid feedback but also to establish a development plan based on your current work role and to think about your long-term future either within the organisation or outside it if necessary. It should motivate you and give you the basis of a personal development plan.

INSTANT TIP

To make the most of the opportunity for feedback from your annual appraisal, it is essential that you prepare thoroughly for it. Gather all the documentation relating to your work role including your job description, CV, results achieved through the year and details of projects you have undertaken.

In addition to the routine appraisal process, you can also request individual feedback from your line manager to help you with a review exercise of this type. This may be daunting but it is likely that your manager will appreciate that you are being proactive and making real efforts to improve your performance. You will have to put your feelings of fear and apprehension to one side and get the feedback that will help you to see where you need to improve.

How to ask for feedback

Some feedback will come to you without your asking for it and this can indeed be useful. However, you will get more benefit if you take a more proactive role in obtaining feedback by asking for it. This may prevent the dispiriting situation of receiving critical feedback when you are no longer able to do something to improve – after you have left a specific work role, for example, or when the task has been finished and you have moved on to something else. You can also request feedback at a time to suit you. For example, if you have set yourself timed goals then you can decide to request feedback according to those goals or you may feel you need feedback on your work role as part of your preparations for an annual salary review. In this case, there would be little point in getting feedback after the reviews have taken place – and the pay increases or promotions given out – so here again, a proactive approach is better. Timing can also be important in that if feedback is obtained at the correct time then you will be able to prepare for it and to plan to tackle the improvements that will usually be necessary following a session of this kind.

Depending on whom you are asking for feedback, your approach can be casual or more formal. For example, if what you want is a few comments from a colleague working alongside you then a chat over coffee might be appropriate but if you want to sit down with your boss and spend some time examining your performance or a specific objective then it would be better to request a meeting, giving some indication of what you need so that they can prepare for the meeting and also allow enough time in their schedule to give your request the attention it needs.

If you have asked your boss for feedback you must prepare for the meeting. Tackle this in two parts:

1. Look at areas where you feel you need to improve. Make notes about results you have achieved and about how you felt things went, what the problems were and so on.
2. Note areas where you feel you have performed well. Prepare to discuss what went right with a project or when you have surpassed expectations so that you can repeat the success.

During a feedback meeting try not to view any criticism personally – remember that this is an opportunity to improve – and make notes about any improvements that are suggested. Also, do not just note down any criticism, but discuss it in as much detail as you can. This will all help you to improve. If you can be subjective about your performance and not get defensive about anything that is said then you will get far more out of such a discussion and your boss is likely to respect you more for such a constructive and professional approach.

If you are getting feedback on your performance from people who report to you, it is just as important that you take a professional approach. Not only do you have your own reputation to maintain and therefore need to present a mature, unemotional front but also remember that you are setting an example to your team. An ideal opportunity to get feedback is a regular team meeting where feedback can be just one item on the agenda. You will need to ask questions such as 'What can be improved?' or 'Where do you feel we should be concentrating our efforts as a team?' Allowing time in the meeting for new ideas to be discussed is also a good idea. It is only by finding out where you are going wrong that you can improve, so don't be afraid to ask hard questions.

Although feedback will often concentrate on the more negative aspects (it is almost always easier to see what is wrong than to see the good things) you should also look for guidance on what you are doing right. What aspects of your performance are particularly strong? What should you be doing more of?

Feedback will be most useful when it is given by someone who can be objective and who is in the right position to judge your performance. Although asking for – and receiving – valid feedback can certainly be daunting do not avoid this task, as feedback is an important way of understanding how you are performing and of improving that performance. Whoever and whenever you ask for feedback it should be frequent, relevant, constructive and timely.

What do you do with feedback when you get it?

The most important thing about feedback is that, having got it, you act on it. Obviously, not all feedback you receive will have been given in a totally unbiased and informed manner. Some people may have their own agenda when passing on comments about your performance and you should bear this in mind. However, most feedback you receive will be beneficial to you if you can make the improvements that are necessary or do more of what you are doing right if this is what the feedback suggests. Feedback can highlight your mistakes and your triumphs. Developing your own self-awareness – a vital skill in managing yourself – will be greatly helped by constructive feedback.

It is important that you accept the feedback in a positive way. There is nothing to be gained by becoming defensive. If you refuse to believe that there is anything you can do to improve then you will never get better at your job and never achieve what you have set your sights on. Do not argue with the person giving the feedback as this will not look professional. Giving reasons why your performance was not as good as it could have been or, worse still, making excuses such as lack of time or other problems you are facing, will not solve the problem and, more to the point, will not win any respect. You will be better able to deal with feedback if you prepare for it. Remember that it can be good or bad and you should resolve to accept it gracefully whichever it is. Listen carefully, noting what has been said and look for the lessons that the other person's experience can give to you. The whole point of feedback is to use it to lead improvements, so denial is not the way to deal with it.

INSTANT TIP

Tempting as it may be to dismiss negative feedback as being untrue or biased, you should always review your performance in the light of feedback. Yes, take into account who has given you the feedback but always be prepared to believe that they are telling the truth as they see it.

However, no amount of feedback and graceful acceptance will improve your performance if you do not evaluate it and then take the appropriate action so in the next section we will look at what you should do to give the feedback you receive the consideration it deserves.

Reflecting on what you find

Having got the feedback in whatever ways you can, you need to reflect on it and take action. Follow these steps to ensure that you benefit from the feedback:

1. Take it seriously – don't just dismiss any criticism you receive that, at first sight, you don't agree with.

2. Don't take it personally. As we said before, it can be difficult to deal with criticism but you must develop a more objective approach if you are to improve.

3. Be honest with yourself. If what you hear is uncomfortable you must look at it honestly and see if there is anything to be gained from the criticism you have just received rather than automatically denying it.

4. Think about the person who is giving the feedback. Do they have a reason (other than what they are saying being true, of course) for criticising you or your performance? What is their motivation? Unless you are sure that they are not telling the whole truth as they see it, you should take their comments seriously.

5. Check the basis for their judgements. The criteria on which people judge can often be different from our own. Did the person giving feedback, for example, expect the same result from your efforts as you did or did they perhaps think that there would be a different outcome?

6. Make sure you have got the feedback you need. It may not be the feedback you want if it involves negative remarks about your performance but not all feedback can, or will, be positive so don't just look for praise. Feedback that tells you where you are going wrong can be far more useful than praise.

If you follow these six steps you can be relatively certain that the feedback is valid and that you must take the appropriate action. The action you take following feedback will, of course, depend on the nature of the feedback and the severity of the problem, where appropriate. If the feedback highlights areas where you are not performing as well as you could, then you will need to make changes. There may be specific skills that you need to brush up on and this will be relatively easy to do. You may find what you need in a course, or in reading up on a subject, or by deliberately looking for opportunities to practise the skill that needs improvement. For example, if you need to delegate more or to communicate better with the people you work with, you should keep the problem in mind as you go about your day-to-day job. In this way you will begin to see tasks you can delegate or you will become aware of shortcomings in communication and the problems caused. You can then look for ways in which these can be remedied. Another way in which you can help yourself when feedback has made you aware of things you need to improve is to ask for specific feedback from others concentrating on that particular problem area to reinforce the information you have received and perhaps to get more advice on how to deal with it.

It could also be that the feedback is overwhelmingly positive. In this case, if you bear in mind the criteria above, and also the fact that some people find it easier to give praise than criticism, you can take this as a green light to do more of what you have been doing and to carry on without changing the way you do things. Knowing what you are doing is right is just as important as knowing what you are doing wrong so don't just ignore any compliments and positive remarks you may receive.

Let's look now at a simple example of how someone asked for and used feedback to improve his performance.

Case study

A young man at the start of his career in a large manufacturing organisation was given the opportunity to present ideas for change in his department to a panel of senior managers. As the other members of his department would also be present he decided to prepare in advance for some feedback. He asked one of his close colleagues to take particular notice of his presentation style and gave him questions to think about as he watched the presentation. These questions were:

- How did the panel react?
- How did he come across?
- Was the delivery too quick, too slow?
- Were the slides effective?
- How could the presentation have been improved?

By preparing in this way, and asking for constructive feedback from a respected colleague, he was given just what he needed to improve his presentation skills. The next time he gave a presentation he made his delivery more slowly and used more slides to illustrate his points more effectively. He also made more eye contact with the people he was presenting to and stopped fiddling with his pen. In this way he improved things about his presentation style that he would not otherwise have been aware of and became a much better and more confident presenter.

Most of the things that you can do when faced with feedback that shows you that improvements are necessary are the same as those activities you will undertake when pursuing personal development – take a course, read a book, practise where necessary and so on.

The important thing with feedback is that you take it with good grace and then reflect on it so that you put yourself in a position where you can improve your performance and your prospects for the future. Taking appropriate action when you act on the feedback is vital.

Finally, after you have received feedback, however you feel about it at the time, try to thank the person who has given it and assure them that you will give it careful consideration. Apart from being good manners, this will also help to ensure that they will be ready to help you again in the future.

SUMMARY

In this chapter we looked at feedback – how you can get it, who should give it and what you should do with it. We saw that it can be useful in changing behaviour and improving performance.

First we assessed who can give useful feedback on your work role. This included your manager, the HR Department, your team and your colleagues. In particular, your boss should give comprehensive feedback during your annual appraisal and also you can ask them and others for both specific and general feedback at any time. Preparing for a meeting where you will get feedback is important so that you can thoroughly review your performance – both good and bad.

Reflecting on feedback is important so that you can then take action. This may involve a range of development activities.

The two most important things to remember about feedback are not to take it too personally and to take action where necessary. It is a useful development and improvement activity.

ACTION CHECKLIST

1. Whose feedback would be most useful to you in your current situation?
2. Plan how you will ask for feedback and prepare for a meeting. Then approach them for general help.
3. Who may be able to help with feedback on a specific task? Approach them and discuss how that task went.
4. Reflect on the feedback you have received. Is it valid? Can you improve?
5. Plan any development activities that have become necessary as a result of the feedback you have received.

09

What are your personal values and how do they affect your career?

Determining your own values can be a useful exercise to help you to understand what you are aiming for in your career – and why. It can also be helpful to know and understand your own value system because working for an organisation whose values are incompatible with yours can be very uncomfortable, if not impossible. Such a clash between your own values and those of the organisation can lead to a poor performance or frustration and unhappiness at work. You may believe, for example, that environmental sustainability is of paramount importance in all areas of life and, if so, would find it difficult to work for an organisation that ignored this aspect of its operations.

It may be useful at this point to define what a 'value' is. It is the belief of an individual, group of people or culture. There are, of course, different types of values such as:

● ethical values
● political values

- religious values
- social values
- aesthetic values.

Although many values that you hold dear will have their roots in your upbringing, your values are not necessarily fixed and may change over time according to what happens in your life. Your education and your working life will also have a huge effect on your values. These values will influence the choices you make throughout your life and will, if you are true to them, decide your priorities in how you deal with people, what you do for a living, the organisations you work for and who you associate with. The closer your values are followed when making life choices such as which career to pursue or the type of organisation you work in, the happier and more fulfilled you are likely to be.

What is important to you?

Values can be many and varied and some will obviously affect how you perform at work more than others. Here are a few examples of values that you may hold – some you may be unaware of until you consciously think about your values. Look through this list and assess the importance of each value to you personally and also decide which ones would have the greatest effect on your career:

- concern for others
- belief in hard work
- perfection
- punctuality
- a need to achieve
- caring for the environment
- charity

- personal independence
- self-respect
- commitment
- patriotism
- social justice
- faith
- helping society
- trust
- adaptability
- loyalty
- forgiveness
- conformity
- equality
- honesty
- creativity
- family life
- affluence
- belonging
- individuality
- democracy
- peace.

The possible list of personal values is almost endless – these are just a few examples. Let's look at some of these values to see what possible effect they could have on your career. Punctuality is an obvious one that can only have a beneficial affect. If you do not care about punctuality – or simply find it a very difficult concept to work into your daily life – then choosing a career where you need to attend a lot of meetings with customers for example may not be a good idea, but a lack of care about punctuality will inevitably lead to issues with anyone who has to supervise you. It will mean that you are late for work and for meetings and may mean that you miss deadlines, causing problems for yourself and all around you who may be relying on your efforts. Another example is that of being particularly creative. This will usually be something that guides your career. Creativity is often associated solely with artistic pursuits but it can also be something that is useful in business – finding creative solutions to problems is an asset in a manager, so it is important to look at all possible aspects of your values. An example of a clash of values affecting the choice of organisation you work for is that if you hold strong democratic values then you will find it difficult if you find yourself working in an organisation that has autocratic values.

It is a good idea to list your personal values and to prioritise them. Some will obviously be more meaningful to you than others and the three or four values that come top of your list will be the ones that it is essential that you take note of in everyday life. Choosing a job, an organisation or even a life partner without taking those vital values into account will store up problems for the future. Sooner or later you will have to change to something that echoes your values so it is best to think about your values as part of your general self-assessment.

Your values can also affect how you behave at work. If you have a problem to solve then it will always work best for you if you find a solution that falls in with your values. If family life is important to you, for example, and a young mother or father comes to you as their manager requesting flexible working hours so that they can care for their children better then it will be advantageous to you – and them, of course – if you can find a way to facilitate the flexible working hours rather than turning their request down without doing your best to find a solution. Values are also important in dealing with awkward people. We will all face situations with people who make life difficult during our working lives, whether it is a boss who is a bully, a customer who is particularly demanding or a colleague who is unkind. How we deal with them should be led by our values. If, for example, you find yourself working alongside someone who lies or cheats to get what she wants you will find it difficult to work well with her if your most important values include honesty and openness. If you are in a position to stop the lying and so on then it will usually be in your interests – or at least will give you peace of mind – if you do so.

So, you have looked at your personal values and have decided that a number of things are important to you. There will be some things that are less important to you than others and some that will be absolutely essential to you. The values that are important to you in your personal life can also have an effect in your working life so understanding them and their possible effect on your career is essential. If, for example, family life is of primary importance to you then it would not be a wise move to enter a career that took you away from home for long periods as this will automatically set up a conflict between your values and your daily life. Similarly, if helping society is one of your priorities then you would be well advised to find a career in an organisation that has that same value. While, in this case, working for a charity or doing social work may be ideal, these are not the only options. You could be just as satisfied in this respect if you work in an organisation that has profit as its main purpose but, along the way, does a lot to help its local community or provides a product that is valued in society. The main thing is to make sure that your values are broadly in harmony with those of the organisation.

When evaluating your choice of career you will find it useful to understand what drives you in terms of your values. You may think that you work simply for material reward, but think more closely and you will find that there are other factors driving you. Do you have a strong desire for security or need high status or autonomy? Ask yourself the following questions to find out what motivates you in your working life:

- What satisfies you in your current job?
- What do you dislike about your current job?
- Which jobs in your current organisation, if any, would you like to be doing in the next few years?
- Do you think you would be good at these jobs – and if so, why?
- What do you envisage is your ideal job?

- How much effort are you prepared to make to achieve your ideal job?
- How much money do you need for your current lifestyle and commitments?
- Will you really need to earn more in the future?
- How important are job titles to you?
- What sort of people would you rather not work with?
- How do you envisage the ideal organisation for you to work in?

It is obvious that your answers to these questions will affect not only your choice of career initially but also how you develop your career, so make sure that you spend sufficient time on this.

As we said earlier, many values can be rooted deep in your upbringing and stay relatively unchanged throughout your life but others may change as your life develops and different things become important to you. For this reason it is a good idea to review what is important to you – and the effect on your career – on a regular basis. Knowing yourself will allow you to make better choices.

Identifying your career and personal goals

If you bought this book solely to find out how you can further your career, you may be wondering why this section includes not only your career goals but also your personal goals. Reviewing the two sets of goals at the same time is important because they are inextricably linked. As we saw earlier in this chapter when looking at values and what is important to you, your work and personal values can overlap and your career and personal life will always overlap and affect each other.

So, how do you go about identifying your goals in both your personal and working lives? In both cases it is important that you understand yourself, what you want out of life and work, your strengths and weaknesses and what is important to you, i.e. your values as discussed above. So your first step should be to examine all these aspects. In addition to your values, which are very important in relation to what you do in the future, you should also look at your personality, your skills and aptitudes, your qualifications and experience, and your family commitments. All of these things will have a bearing on where you are able to go in both your personal and working lives and also will affect your preferences. Let's look at these one by one in a little more detail.

Values

As discussed earlier in this chapter, your values will affect every area of your life. Values are particularly important in the balance between your home life and your life at work. Depending on the importance you place on the different areas of your life, you will give more prominence to one or the other. So, if you view your career as being all-important at this stage in your life you will obviously put more effort into developing your working life and therefore building a satisfying home life may have to wait a while. It is vital that your values are taken into account when setting goals in your life as, if a choice that does not fit with your values is made, then you may not achieve either success or happiness. Having looked carefully at your values, ask yourself what you are aiming for your career or home life to bring to you. For example, do you want status, financial security, fame, children, a stable home environment, to see the world?

Personality

Your personality will affect your job and your personal life in many ways and knowing yourself will make it much easier to set meaningful goals in both areas. Are you, for example, a morning person or do you work better at night? Do you find it easy to keep yourself motivated? Do you like to work alone or as part of a team? Consider all aspects of your personality and keep them in mind when setting your goals.

Skills and aptitudes

Assess your skills so that you know what careers are possible with your current skills and also what areas need improvement. If you are struggling to decide exactly what your abilities are, take a look at your achievements. What have you done well? What comes easily to you? What do you enjoy doing?

Qualifications

Your qualifications can give you a head start in some careers or they can rule out others because they are not at a high enough level or not in the right subject areas. Make sure you have a list of your own qualifications to hand when setting goals. It may be that you will decide that improving your qualifications is one of your goals. You can certainly make yourself more employable or put yourself in the right position for taking up a new career if you can gain the right qualifications. Improving your education can be a great source of personal satisfaction. Finding a job with a better salary, status or conditions may well be possible with a higher degree and this may mesh with your values as discussed earlier.

Of course, having listed your qualifications you will need to research the jobs you are aiming for and find out the qualifications that will be required to get yourself into a position to change jobs.

Interests

Your interests may well give you a few pointers as to what your goals should be. If your interests are mainly creative then that should be reflected in your choice of career. If you are not able to utilise your creative abilities in your work situation then dissatisfaction may be the result. In contrast, you may find that the majority of your time outside work is spent on physical pursuits. This may be a reaction to the fact that you are sitting down at work all day and this shows that you are gaining a balance in your life, but it could also point you in a direction for a career change to something that fulfils your need for physical effort. An examination of your interests will also show you how social you are. Do you need to be surrounded by people or are you happy with your own company? Whatever your interests, they will give you clues as to what you really want out of life.

Experience

Your experience is relevant to your goals as it will be, in effect, a qualification that you can take to future employers. You should try to make the most of your previous experience when setting your goals for the future. You may also need to broaden your experience in the future if you spot gaps in your experience to date.

Family commitments

The time you spend with your family – by choice or by necessity – will affect your goals, at least in the short term. For example, if you plan to work part time for the next few years while your children are growing up or are unable to be away from home because of looking after elderly relatives, then this will limit the amount of time you are able to devote to your job while those commitments continue. In this case you will need to tailor your goals so that you do what you can in terms of development for the time that those commitments are still your priority. Then, over time, you will no doubt find that your priorities change and you are able to set different goals according to the time you are able to spend at work or studying and so on.

As you can see, many different things in your life, both at home and at work, and in the past, present and future will need to be taken into account when considering what your goals can be. It may be useful at this stage of your investigation into just who you are, to take a look at all your lists of skills, qualifications, values and so on and try to distil the information about yourself into just a few words. Use no more than one sentence to sum yourself up. Usually, this will be in relation to your working life so, for example, you may say 'I'm a hardworking, reliable accountant who has the ability to solve problems' or 'I'm a Spanish-speaking sales person who has produced exceptional results in overseas sales negotiations'. This summary may change from time to time according to the purpose for which it is being used and will prove useful in a number of situations such as:

- when introducing yourself to possible employers
- at networking events
- as an introduction in any work situation
- on your CV.

This summary will help you to become focused on just who you are and what you have to offer.

As we have said, knowing yourself is the first step in identifying your goals and consideration of the areas described above, will help with this. You need to use this information to decide where you want to be in the future. Look around you in your own organisation so that you know what jobs there are to aspire to and look at the people doing those jobs. Ask yourself what they have that you don't – is it simply a matter of experience or do they have different skills and qualifications? Or perhaps a different approach to work? This may highlight your own shortcomings and show you what you need to include in your goals in terms of self-development. This may be taking courses to improve your qualifications, for example, or planning for the future so that you are able to devote more time or effort to your career. From this examination of yourself and others, you should arrive at a list of objectives and then you need to take action to achieve them.

Relating your values to your career goals

Careful consideration of the personal attitudes that influence your decisions – your values – is vital when deciding on your goals. There are some that will be especially relevant to your career goals as they will affect your job satisfaction and may determine the type of job you aim for or the organisation for which you choose to work. Consider things such as:

- the financial rewards you want or need
- the status a career offers
- how much of a challenge a job would present
- whether you want to manage others

- how important helping others and contributing to society is to you
- the job security offered
- whether you want to work as part of a team or to work alone
- whether you want to work with the public.

All of these things will help you to make sure that you choose a career path that will not conflict with your values. You will also need to ensure that the needs dictated by your values are balanced with the physical needs that you have identified. For example, helping others may be important to you but if pay in the charity sector in your area is low then you may need to give a higher priority to the salary you can achieve in another type of organisation to ensure that you meet your family commitments.

As we have said, it is important that you avoid a clash between your own values and those of the organisation that you work for. If you especially value honesty and integrity then you will never be entirely happy or comfortable working in an organisation that regularly covers up the truth. When looking for an organisation's values, you can start with the stated values in the organisation's mission statement, if available. However, you should be aware that the behaviour of an organisation does not always live up to the mission statement, as this may be viewed sometimes as a public relations exercise or a 'wish list' rather than something to actually implement. For this reason, you will have to delve deeper than stated values and examine actual behaviour. Quite often how outsiders – customers, suppliers and so on – view the organisation is a good indicator of its values. This is its reputation. Also, you can check out the company's website for clues and ask what other employees see as the organisation's values. While it is often impossible to find a job in an organisation whose values completely mirror your own, you should aim to avoid any obvious clashes. It is important to take the organisation's values into account and to try to match them as closely as is practicable as, if you don't you will inevitably feel dissatisfied and ultimately fail to achieve success.

Giving careful consideration to your values and taking into account all your skills and attributes is an essential part of managing yourself, so be prepared to spend some time on this exercise and do not expect to be able to complete your list of career goals in one sitting. It may be that a session with a career counsellor or with your mentor at work, plus chats with your family, will help you a lot in this process.

SUMMARY

This chapter covered your personal values and how they affect your career choice and performance.

First we looked at what values are (beliefs that are important to you) and at how you can decide what your values are. These values could be ethical, political, religious, social and aesthetic.

Next we looked at how your values will affect how you behave at work and how you make choices about what sort of organisation you work in. It is important that your values and those of the organisation do not clash.

We saw how the values that are important to you can have strong motivational effects and will affect your career development.

Values were seen to be important when identifying your goals – in both your personal life and in your career. Values must be considered alongside aspects such as your personality, skills, attitudes, qualifications, experience, interests and family commitments when setting goals. It can be useful to distil all this information about yourself into a sentence that sums you up to use when meeting possible employers, on your CV and when networking.

Finally in this chapter, we looked at how your values should be related to your career goals so that your career path does not conflict with your values.

ACTION CHECKLIST

1. Decide on one value that you hold in each of the categories – ethical, political, religious, social and aesthetic.
2. Relate these values to choices you have made in your personal and working lives. How have they affected your choices?
3. Consider the values of the organisation you work for. Is there any conflict with your values?
4. How will your values affect your goals?
5. Write down a few words that sum up your values and all your attributes from a career point of view.

10

Can networking help you in your work role?

Networking can definitely assist you at work. It should be considered part of your Continuing Professional Development (for more on this look at Chapter 5). It will help you to develop a growing network of contacts that will help you in your work role and also further your career. The benefits that you may get from this network of contacts can include:

- a raised personal profile
- ideas from others involved in similar fields
- more customers for your organisation
- the latest information about your area of business
- sales leads
- mentoring
- career opportunities
- raise the profile of your organisation

In addition to all the benefits above, networking can broaden your outlook and increase your understanding of your industry. Being in touch with a lot of people from different industries and at different levels will ensure that you are aware of what is going on and of the opportunities that are out there for you. If you don't know about job opportunities and developments in the business world, you will not be able to take advantage of them.

What is networking?

Networking is another skill that you can learn that, as we saw in the previous section, can help you in all sorts of ways. In short, it is a way of making contact with others to gain – and give – support and help. You will already have done a certain amount of networking – whether or not you are aware of it. Think about it. Has anyone ever said to you 'There's a job where I work that would suit you' or 'Did you see that job advertised in the paper?' or 'I could lend you a book about that, you'll find it interesting'? That's networking. Doing it with a purpose, in a more focused way will provide you with lots of benefits including relevant information about your working world.

There are techniques that can be learned that will ensure that when you meet people for the first time and then subsequently, you present yourself in a positive way. This then has the potential to lead to benefits in your life both at work and outside work. In a work situation this could mean, for example, that your networking contacts are able to introduce you to someone who is in need of an individual with your skills or to an organisation that would like to do business with your organisation. The important thing is that networking works best when the relationships formed are reciprocal. A sort of 'you scratch my back, I'll scratch yours' situation.

There are all sorts of information and assistance that can be gained by networking. These include:

● increased business for your organisation
● an improved reputation and higher profile in your local area
● advice on general business matters

- information about new developments in your industry
- new products on the market
- information on new laws and regulations that apply to your industry
- details of new suppliers
- relevant job opportunities
- training opportunities.

There is no great mystery about networking, as we said previously it is something that we will already be doing even if we are unaware of it. Mostly, it involves listening to people – and everyone likes to be listened to. In business you will need to ensure you are networking with a purpose so that you are focused, rather than just letting it happen to you as you may have done in the past, to meet people who are relevant to your purpose and to take every opportunity to bring out your strengths in conversation where they are relevant to what you want from that encounter.

As you can see, networking is an activity that can have benefits for both you in your work role and career and also for your organisation. You can use it as a source of support and information that is almost infinite. It is as useful as you want to make it and depends very much on the effort you want to put into the activity.

Networking with a purpose

As with any sort of skill or task, networking will always work better if your purpose is clear. Some people network to find clients, others will be looking for knowledge or assistance and others may be looking for a job opportunity.

So, for your networking to be effective, it is always better to set objectives. Your objective may change not only who you approach but also how you approach them – what you say and how you stay in touch, for example.

In setting your networking objectives, you should consider:

- Are you looking to increase sales for your organisation?
- Are you looking to increase awareness of your organisation?
- Do you want to raise your own profile?
- Do you want information about your industry?
- Do you want to make contact with overseas organisations?
- Are you interested in benchmarking to improve the performance of your organisation?
- Are you looking for job opportunities?
- Can you spare the time to attend regular meetings?
- Are you looking for training opportunities?
- Do you want to increase your knowledge and skills in a specific area?
- Are you looking for expert advice?

As you can see, you need to be clear about exactly what you want from networking because it may affect how you network and where you concentrate your networking activities.

Types of networking

Having set your objective, you will know just what you want to get from your networking efforts and this will govern the way you go about networking. It will help at this stage to look briefly at the different ways in which you might network to achieve your goal.

Networking can be broken down into two main areas – informal and formal, so let's look at how you might tackle these areas.

Informal networking

One of the most important things to remember about networking is that it can be done anywhere, at any time. The key is to start looking for the opportunities and always be ready to network. An example of this could be in a social situation. You're standing at the bar, waiting to pay, and standing next to someone you don't know. Can you strike up a conversation? And if you find out that you have something in common, could you give him your business card (you do keep a supply of your business cards with you all the time, even outside working hours, don't you?) and then perhaps get his contact details? The first step in this process is the most difficult, of course, but you should be alert to opportunities to network all the time. Most people feel uncomfortable approaching strangers but if you want to get results you will have to get over this fear. An organised approach will help with this.

First consider your objective for the contact so that you know why you are approaching this person – as we said earlier in this chapter, your objective may affect what you say about yourself. Next prepare a short description of yourself, based on what your objective is – this is known as an 'elevator speech'. (Note that this will also prove invaluable in many formal networking situations.) This is a prepared presentation lasting only a minute or so that will grab attention and explain what you do. Knowing that first impressions count, it is important that you craft this speech carefully and become very familiar with it. It should describe what you do but, in order to get some attention, it should not be a simple statement of your occupation but rather you should try to present what you do as a solution. For example, when asked the perennial networking question of 'And what do you do?' don't just say 'I'm a computer engineer', try 'I help people who have problems with their computers'. This approach is far more likely to arouse interest. Haven't you noticed that when you tell people your occupation the usual response is a reserved 'Oh, that's nice'? You need something that will make them relate it to their own situation and engage with you in conversation.

To craft your elevator speech – either for yourself or for your organisation – start by thinking about the types of people you may be addressing it to. Think about the problems they may have and how you could solve those problems. This speech can then be delivered to anyone you meet who is a possible networking contact for you and who is prepared to listen for the short length of time that it takes. Don't worry that in the beginning your elevator speech sounds strange to you, just keep practising and it will become second nature to you. Deliver it to as many informal contacts as you can and you will get results.

So, as we can see, informal networking is done whenever the opportunity is there rather than, as is the case with formal networking, doing something or going somewhere with the specific aim of increasing or developing a network of contacts.

Formal networking

In contrast to informal networking, which often takes place in social situations and mainly relies on opportunism, formal networking is planned and can be targeted much more closely so that your objective becomes clearer and more important. There are several different types of formal networking and you can, of course, choose the one, or ones, that will best serve your purpose. The types usually involve different venues and areas of interest and can include the following.

Networking events
At these events, and indeed in other networking situations, you may meet others in a similar position to yourself as well as people who are in a position to which you may aspire. They may be customers, suppliers or competitors of your own organisation as

well as people with whom you have previously had no connection of any sort and at these formal events the aims of the other attendees will be similar to yours. It is at these events that the purpose of networking can become very clear and attending several of these at the beginning of your networking efforts will help you to appreciate the reciprocal nature of networking.

You will find that there is a choice of networking organisations that you can join and you will make your choice according to your objective as well as the convenience and quality of the event and its venue. Asking your current network of contacts for recommendations is a good way of finding suitable networks.

Networking clubs and groups will cover a wide range of interests and will be run in many different ways. Some will be mainly for small businesses, others will cater for larger enterprises and some will be run exclusively for the public sector or for a specific industry and still others will cater for women only. There will also be differences in the timings and frequency of the events. Some will meet for breakfast, some for lunch and others for an evening meal or for an early evening meeting and these meetings may be anything from quarterly to weekly. Some may demand a large annual fee while others will cost very little. The key is to choose one or two that fit in with your style, your business requirements and your availability.

Conferences

Attending conferences in your area of interest will provide you with many opportunities to make contact with people with similar interests. There will often be refreshment breaks when you must make conversation with other delegates and these opportunities must not be wasted. Make sure that you have your elevator speech ready and a good supply of business cards.

Membership of organisations

Investigating just what the professional organisation of which you are a member can offer in terms of networking will give you a number of options. You and your employers may belong to a variety of organisations, all of which may provide opportunities for networking. These may include:

- Trade associations – these will be able to put you in touch with organisations in the same business as yours or with businesses who offer the services you may be looking for.
- Chambers of commerce – there will be networking opportunities at events the chamber may organise and also advice on all sorts of employment and business issues.
- Employers' federations – these will be able to provide advice on best practice in employment.
- Trades unions – these can be a source of advice and of training opportunities.
- Professional organisations – you may be a member of an association or chartered institute because of your occupation or the qualifications you have obtained.
- Community organisations – these are often founded on a particular issue. This might include local development, charities or ethnic interests.

You will find many of these organisations in directories, trade journals and by searching on the internet. Many of them, of course, will be making efforts to find you to offer their services and membership where appropriate.

Online
There is an enormous variety of online networking forums that you can join and care must be taken to avoid spending too much time on them without producing the results you are aiming at. Online networking is ideal for people who cannot – or do not want to – spend time attending events. It is also possible with online networking to take part in a less reciprocal way because of the

anonymity offered by the online environment. If what you want is information on a specific topic then it is easy to get via an internet forum without having to build a relationship or feel an obligation to the person supplying the information.

Online networking forums are also ideal for discussion on a variety of topics so that you can bring yourself up to date with current trends and practices within your industry. There are three ways of finding an appropriate networking forum online:

1. By recommendation – ask around among your existing network of contacts. What do they do with online forums and how do they do it?
2. Using a search engine – simply go online and put a search term such as 'online networking for business' in your usual search engine and see what it brings up. You will probably be surprised at the depth of choice.
3. Try www.managers.org.uk/practical-support/ management-community – the Chartered Management Institute's online forum.

As you can see, there is an enormous choice of networking opportunities that you can join and use. Finding the most appropriate ones and then making the most of them will be your objective.

Case study

A young entrepreneur used mentors not only to help her make more money in her lettings business but also to save money. She took the view that mentors were an ideal way to learn from someone more experienced than herself and felt that by using others' experiences she could avoid costly mistakes in her business. She used her networking contacts to find a number of mentors in different fields. A former boss mentored her in expanding her lettings business, a man she met at a business networking event showed her how she could improve the marketing of her business and someone who she was referred to by her local Chamber of Commerce helped with strategic planning.

By improving her marketing efforts, awareness of her business in her area was increased so her profits increased. Added to this she saved money in two ways:

1. She received valuable business advice for nothing – if she had paid for a marketing consultant she would have had to pay several hundred pounds.
2. She avoided costly errors in planning for the future of her business.

In addition, in some cases her mentors also introduced her to their own networks, increasing her valuable pool of contacts.

She commented: 'Without all my network contacts, my business would not be as successful as it is. Networking is a must for any business. Eventually I hope to be able to help other young entrepreneurs in return.'

The importance of confidentiality

Confidentiality in all business dealings is essential as it will promote trust, confidence and respect. In networking it is especially important that you keep any sensitive information that you are given to yourself as good networking relationships are built on trust and respect. Remember also that you are forming opinions – sometimes on first meeting – and these should also be kept to yourself. It is impossible to know who you will meet in the future or who will meet whom so if you are indiscreet, word will get round and you may well find yourself in a difficult position without fully understanding what has happened. So, go to the events, meet and talk with as many people as you can, make your notes following the event – but keep it to yourself.

When you are passing on contact details of people who you think could help others that you know, check before you do so that this is acceptable to the person involved. This is a matter of politeness but will also show that you are being discreet. There will be times when information you are given can be shared but before you do so you should be completely sure that this will not be a problem. It is easy to get a reputation for indiscretion and difficult to win back trust once it is lost.

SUMMARY

This chapter is the first of two dealing with how networking can help you in your work role and in your career. The benefits of networking include getting ideas and information from others working in similar fields, getting sales leads and customers for your organisation, mentoring and career opportunities, and raising the profiles of both your organisation and yourself.

Networking was seen to be a way of making contact with others who may be able to help you in some way and is reciprocal in nature. We also saw how you can network with a purpose – an objective can affect how and where you network.

We then looked at the different types of networking and how they can be carried out. The types included informal, which can be done almost anywhere, or formal, where networking is planned and often facilitated at events such as lunches, professional and trade association meetings and conferences and online networking.

The importance of confidentiality in all dealings in networking was emphasised.

ACTION CHECKLIST

1. How do you think networking could best help you in your current work role?
2. Consider your own profile in the industry in which you work. Do you think networking could help with this?
3. Decide upon the most important reasons why you might need to network. These reasons will form your purposes for networking.
4. Find an online networking site that would be relevant to your work role.
5. Consider how networking may be able to help you in your future career development.

11

How can you develop your personal networks?

Developing your network can be done in a number of ways and will depend on the type of networking you intend to do. Building your personal networks informally just requires an awareness of the opportunities that are all around you and the willingness to 'just do it'.

Building your networks through more formal methods of networking demands time and effort in terms of finding the most appropriate network organisations for you and then attending the networking events. Let's look briefly at the various ways in which you may find the right networks for your purposes:

- Recommendation – this is one of the best ways to find networks that will work for you. Colleagues, friends and people you deal with in business such as suppliers, your accountant and bank manager may all be sources of information.
- Chambers of Commerce – they may run regular networking events and will usually know of other networks in the area.

- Trade magazines and local newspapers may carry advertisements or articles about appropriate networks.
- Searching on the internet.

However you choose to develop your networks it is something that requires time and effort that will be repaid in terms of the benefits networks can bring to your work role, your career and to your organisation. But do you know who is already in your network?

Who is in your current network?

Before you go off spending lots of time, effort and perhaps money on developing a network of contacts it is advisable to consider carefully just who is in your current network. You may think that you don't know many people or that you don't know anyone important. Consider all the people in your organisation then add in all the people you meet from other organisations. Don't forget the people with whom you may only have contact over the phone or via email or even in social networks such as Facebook or Twitter. So, if you were to write down the names of all the people you currently know you may get a surprise as to how many people there are on your list. Also, there is the 'six degrees of separation' effect. This theory says that we are all connected to everyone else by a chain of people we know that is no longer than just five links. So, it's not just who you know but who those people know and so on. In just five links you could be put in touch with just about anyone.

So, write that list. Note everyone you know – family, friends, neighbours, work colleagues, past work colleagues, acquaintances, and don't forget to include people you deal with in both your work and personal lives such as your hairdresser, gym manager, suppliers, customers – even your window cleaner – and also note what they do for a living, interests, hobbies, where they live and so on. Your aim is to capture details of all the possible sources of help that you might already have in your current network.

Next you should examine this list and give some thought as to what resources you have at your disposal in your network, bearing in mind your current and possible future requirements. You should also give consideration as to how you may be able to help your contacts so that you will have a clear conscience if you need to ask a favour of them in the future – that is the reciprocal nature of networking. Don't rule out anybody at this stage as networking is unpredictable and don't forget the 'six degrees of separation' effect that we mentioned earlier – you don't know who they know. You may think, for example, that your neighbour is not a useful contact as you know he is in a job that does not appear to have any connection to your own but don't miss him off your list. He may know – or be related to, for all you know – someone in an influential position in a large organisation that would be ideal for you. Or he may meet just that person tomorrow and if he isn't aware of your capabilities and your wish to move jobs, he will not be in a position to help you. So, make your list of contacts comprehensive. One cautionary word here, no matter who is in your list of contacts, do not be tempted to ask directly for a job even if that is precisely what you are looking for. Just make it known that you are looking and what you have to offer and let the networking principle do the rest.

Deciding who should be in your future networks

Your list of all the people in your current network may have shown you that you already know a lot of people and it may also have thrown up a few names of people who you would consider will have really good potential. You now need to decide what sort of people will be in your network in the future. This will inform the choice of networks that you join and how you tackle networking. Making this decision requires careful consideration of your reason for networking. We have already discussed networking with a purpose and it is this purpose that is important in who forms your networks. So, what did you decide is your main purpose for networking? Is it to gain information and advice? If so, then you would do well to seek out specialist networking events and organisations where you will meet experts in your field, or business advisers who can help you. If your main purpose is to increase business for your organisation, then look for the networks that your competitors use or general networking events where you can meet a wide variety of people. Finally, if your purpose is to develop your career and you are looking for a job move, then remember that most employers start their search for new employees in their own existing networks. This is because they consider this to be the easiest and most reliable way of recruiting. Someone who comes from their own network – even if the connection is quite tenuous – will be seen as a safer option than recruiting a stranger by advertising and, of course, it will be less expensive and time consuming than advertising or going to a recruitment specialist. So, they will ask trusted employees if they know of anyone suitable or they may ask business colleagues in other organisations for recommendations. This is when you need to be networking as widely as possible so that you are in touch with lots of people from other organisations. You will need to make it known that you are looking for a move and to give people the information they need about what you are looking for and what you have to offer. In this way you may find yourself in the network of a future employer and ideally placed to get the job you want.

Getting involved

To make the most of a business network it is essential that you are an active member. Networks are most useful if as many people as possible take an active part and develop reciprocal relationships with one another. The more active the members of a network are, the better the reputation of that network will be and the improvement will be self-perpetuating.

It is the reciprocal nature of networking that will ensure the success of a network. If all the participants are willing to pass on advice, leads, expertise and so on to each other then everyone will benefit. So, if you receive advice or some other form of help or support from a member of a network then you should be prepared to help them in some way. You should actively look for ways to help your fellow members on the understanding that they will be doing the same for you.

Even before you have attended any networking events it is helpful to prepare for it by giving some thought not only to what you are hoping to gain from networking but also to what you may be able to offer to your fellow members. The first step in deciding what you have to offer is careful consideration of your current network. Do you know a recruitment consultant, for example? If so, that could be a useful name to pass on to anyone you meet who may be looking to change jobs. Or if you know anyone who is an expert in any field then they could be useful to others. Can you recommend your accountant, your hairdresser or car repair specialist? With some thought you may be surprised by just who you know and how they could help others.

Going to your first networking event can, for many people, be a challenging time. There are very few people – even in high positions in business – who feel totally confident when walking into a room full of complete strangers. But if you want to increase your networks and gain the benefits that come from successful networking, it has to be done. As always, there are ways to make life easier. If you start with an objective – a realistic objective – for any networking event, including your first, then you will be focused rather than having the vague idea of 'I'm going to network.' Perhaps you will set yourself the target of meeting and exchanging contact details with just two people. Even if you don't feel completely comfortable doing that, it is quite likely that you will achieve your objective within a short space of time and will then relax. Then you will be able to chat with a few people and really start to understand the nature of networking. But how do you approach those first two people? If you can see anyone standing alone then gather your courage and introduce yourself. A simple introduction of your name and a handshake is OK but it is a good idea to follow this quickly with a question such as 'Have you been to one of these events before?' or 'Can I ask you what you do?' This will start a conversation and you're halfway to your objective. The aim really is to find something you have in common – perhaps you're both new to networking, or both are in sales or a particular industry, or have simply had a difficult journey to the event. Once you get talking you will be surprised by how much you can learn.

Now let's have a brief look at a few things you can do to help you overcome the negative feelings you may have about your first networking event:

- Remember that you are investing precious time in networking so you must make sure that this time is not wasted. You must get some benefit from it.
- Believe in yourself. Remind yourself about what you have to offer and go into the event with a positive attitude.
- Realise that everyone is there to gain from the networking event so they want to meet you just as much as you want to meet them.
- The vast majority of people will be pleasant and welcoming so do not be reticent about introducing yourself.

- If you do happen to meet someone who you find unpleasant or bad-mannered, move on quickly.
- Resolve to make life easy for yourself by approaching people who are alone or who seem open to your approach. People not already talking to someone will welcome you making the first move.
- Make sure you have all the facts about the event – timings, how to get there, dress code, the type of event and also what sort/how many attendees there will be. A casual chat with the organisers will give you most of these details.

The key is to be prepared as this will ensure that your confidence levels will be high. Having taken care of all the details and the preparation you will be able to concentrate on making the most of the opportunities that the event will offer you. Your main task, apart from making contacts, is to ensure that you give them your details and that they are aware of your skills and knowledge and can see the benefits of networking with you.

Your next move in networking after attending your first event or two, apart from keeping your network records updated, is to plan which events you will attend. It may be that the first type of event you tried was not very productive for you or just not quite right in terms of the other attendees. With the experience you have gained you can now assess other networking events to target the ones that will be best for you and give you the best chance of achieving your objective.

Making use of your networks

Remember that networking events should be used as a business and personal development opportunity so making the most of the opportunities presented is vital. You need to put yourself in a position where you can take advantage of the referrals, information and recommendations that will come out of a successful networking event.

Even if you manage to collect contact details from every single new person you meet, if you do not follow up then all your efforts may have been for nothing. So, how can you make use of all those business cards? Your first step should be to get organised. Don't just dump all those cards in a drawer or even just file them in alphabetical order. You need to develop a system to capture all the information you have about a person. Even though you may only have a business card, don't think that you just have their contact details and nothing else. In most cases you will have found out far more about someone you meet, however briefly, than their name and telephone number, so you need a way of keeping these details in an accessible and useful format. Don't think that you will remember everything you found out. You won't. No matter how vivid they seem in your memory as you are driving away from a networking event or as you're chatting to a person on a train, your memory will quickly fade and confusion will set in.

Many people use a specially designed, computerised contacts system but a simple spreadsheet or database will serve your purpose. The object is to capture as much as possible of what you have found out about the person who may be useful to you in the future. So, as soon as possible after obtaining the details it is essential that you put those details into your contacts system. Start with their name, company, telephone number and so on but also search your memory for all the other details that always come up in even a very brief conversation. This could include, among other nuggets of information:

- Nickname or how they like to be addressed – her business card may state she is called Victoria, for example, but she may like to be addressed as Tori or Vicky or Vic or something completely different.

- Extra contact details – home telephone number and address, email address, do they use Facebook or Twitter?
- Are they members of any other networking organisations?
- Appearance – include approximate age and height, hair colour and so on.
- Background – are their parents still alive, where were they born and brought up, what sort of education have they had and so on.
- Where you met – this can help to put someone into context and also to aid your memory.
- Do they network? If they network regularly in other networking organisations, then their network of contacts could be huge.
- Family details, spouse or partner's name, children and so on.
- Hobbies – even if their hobbies do not hold any interest for you, write them down as they may prove useful in the future.
- Holidays – where do they usually go, where would they like to go?
- Previous work experience – where have they worked before, what was their career path?
- Position in company – who do they report to, how many people report to them, any comments regarding future aspirations?
- Current work projects.
- Work problems.
- Work specialities and interests.
- Anything unusual you noticed about them – are they particularly sensitive about any topic, for example, or nervous, over-confident, loud or very quiet and so on.
- Your own impressions.
- Any ideas you have about how they may be able to help you in the future.

Many of these details will seem trivial and irrelevant but note them down anyway as they may not only help you to recall the person when necessary but also could provide a point of contact or be useful in a conversation at some future date. Remember that these notes are for your eyes only so you can put down anything that occurs to you about the person but remember to keep them confidential.

At this stage – after only one meeting – try to keep an open mind. You may think, as you go through these notes trying to recall details about the person you have met, that they are not going to be useful to you so you could save a bit of time by not including them in your network of contacts but try not to assume anything. This is a lazy approach and will not allow you to make the most of the potential of your networking. It is in the very nature of networking that you never know what an initial contact has to offer and, just as importantly, you do not know who they know. Someone they could introduce you to could be just the person to turn your career around or to give you the largest order you will ever take. In addition, what you need now will undoubtedly not be what you need in a few years' time. Your priorities will change over time and it may be that the person you have just met will become very important to you in years to come.

Having made these notes, you must now follow up on your meetings. After a few days it is appropriate to make contact with the people you have met. A handwritten note is by far the best method. Emails may be easy to send – especially if you have a large quantity of people to send follow-ups to – but they are also very easy to delete and while a letter may be thrown away as soon as received, it is far more likely to be read and appreciated. Your aim is to establish yourself as an individual's contact so your letter or note could include:

- a reminder of where you met
- a comment about the event
- a comment about something that you discussed

- thanks for any information or advice that was given
- your own contact details.

You could also end with something general such as 'good luck for the future' and hoping that you will meet again or, if possible, referring to something that was said such as an imminent birth or major project.

Having made – and followed up – the initial meeting your next move is to establish yourself as a useful contact. Look out for ways that you can help each of the people in your network or reasons to get back in touch. Having sent a handwritten note as your first follow up it is now appropriate to use easier means of communication. You may give them a call or drop them an email for any number of reasons. This may include:

- an article that would be of interest to them
- another networking group that it may be appropriate for them to join
- a website that could prove useful
- a comment on an article or announcement about their company
- a conference coming up that they may like to attend
- a meeting with a mutual acquaintance – or someone working in their company
- congratulations about a job promotion that you may have heard about
- news about yourself – tread carefully here as you must be sure that it will be of interest (even if only slightly) to your contact
- comments about shared interests – sports, hobbies, current affairs, etc. may fall into this category.

As you can see, the reasons that you can make contact with someone, and in the process remind them that you exist, are very varied and a bit of creativity about this will go a long way. Think about the person and you will find your own reasons to keep in touch.

One of the major ways of helping a contact in your network and at the same time furthering your networking is to put people in touch with each other. This may help two people you know while at the same time making both of them feel that they need to be just as helpful to you. It is vital when doing this sort of 'matchmaking' that you let both of the people involved know that you are doing this. Some people view unsolicited phone calls or other forms of contact as intrusive and unwelcome, so it is always better to warn them to expect a call and also it reinforces the idea that you are trying to help.

One important way to make good use of your network is to find a mentor – or mentors, you don't have to limit yourself just one – among the contacts that are in your network. (There is more about finding a mentor in Chapter 4.) Although your current manager may play a mentoring role on some level in your working life, you will also need to look elsewhere for effective mentoring opportunities that will take a wider view so that you can get an unbiased view of your work situation. You will have to look into your network and see if there is anyone there who can offer you some help. First, look for someone with whom you feel you have a natural rapport. Some people you will find especially easy to talk to so consider these people in your initial search. Next, you must consider just how they can help. Of course, what you are looking for will affect this but in the first instance you may need a general mentor. This will usually be someone in a more senior position to you, who will have more business and life experience and who has plenty of contacts in their network.

If you want to approach a potential mentor, do so with care. It is better that you have developed a relationship first so that you can, eventually, come to view the individual as a mentor. When you are at the point where you are ready to broach the subject of mentoring make sure you emphasise the respect you have for the potential mentor and for their position. Remember that, as they are likely to hold a senior position, they will have little time to spare. Make your case clearly and reassure them that you will listen to any advice they may give you and are prepared to put in the effort to progress your career.

Remember that you can have more than one person playing a mentoring role for you so you may have to develop this sort of relationship with people who can help in specific areas. With a number of mentors you will have the benefit of wider expertise and different levels of experience. It's also useful to note that you may outgrow mentors as you progress through your career, but never forget those who helped you. You may find, for example, that you will go to a particular mentor for advice about progression in your career as they have had a long and varied career but will approach others for information about your particular industry.

Finally, in this section about making use of your network, let's look at following up when someone in your network has helped you. They may have put you in touch with someone who knew someone who then interviewed you for a job or was able to give you some information you were looking for or perhaps a sales lead for your organisation. Whatever the assistance they have been able to give you it is important that you acknowledge it and keep your original contact in the picture. If, for example, you're able to arrange an interview with your networking contact's contact make sure that you let them know the date and thank them for their help. Of course, if you ultimately get a job offer, for example, then a thank you note, and maybe a small gift, would be in order.

This last point illustrates a vital element of networking – keeping in touch. The more you keep in touch, help people, supply information and assistance, the better your network will work for you. For instance, receiving a thank you note will give your contact the satisfaction of having helped someone and it will prompt the contact to keep doing it. The networking system will grow and more people will be helped. So, frequent and appropriate contact will make your networking successful.

Networking for your future

Any form of networking will increase the number of contacts you have and will therefore be a potential source of help in the future, but if you are networking specifically to develop your career then you may need to adjust your approach and focus on the parts of your networking efforts that will produce people who can help you to change job and so on.

The first thing to check is your 'elevator speech'. It must be focused on you and what you have to offer. Next you will have to direct your efforts to get what you want. Do you want to find a better job in the same industry, a similar job in another industry to broaden your experience, or a complete change of career? Knowing just what you want will show you which people in your network can help. Any approaches you make in terms of getting a new job must be careful and considered. Rather than asking directly for a job, it is better to ask for advice or information. This lets your contact know that you are looking for a job without putting them under any pressure or obligation. Keeping things informal and friendly will help to get you where you want to be.

Another way in which networking can help your future career is in preparing you for interviews and giving you a wealth of information that you may use in the future. Discussions with lots of people about your industry, market trends and so on will mean you are more informed and will not only be able to bring this knowledge into play in your work role but will also make you more impressive in interviews. Being able to make intelligent conversation with a variety of people is an invaluable skill.

Case study

A young woman working in the beauty industry who was an experienced networker was looking for a change of career. She attended an event that she knew a contact in the field she wanted to enter would also be attending and gave her prepared speech about what she wanted: 'I'm thinking of moving out of sales and more into the marketing side of things. Still in beauty products but more office-based with an emphasis on product development and launching new products. I know you're in marketing yourself, do you have any advice for me?'

This opening for her job search via her networks ensured that she let her contacts know what she was looking for without directly asking for a job or a referral.

After a short conversation about why she wanted a move, her contact told her he would get a friend of his to get in touch with her. After a few days, she had a call from a recruitment specialist with whom she had an interview and this led to her finding out about several vacancies that she would not otherwise have discovered.

As we have seen, networking can be a useful career development activity and, if practised in a focused way, can lead to an increase in industry knowledge, sales leads and lots of information that will be useful in any job. It is also extremely useful if you want to change your career. There are, in broad terms, only three ways to change jobs:

1. To apply for an advertised job.
2. To make yourself known to an organisation who is looking for someone with your skills and capabilities.
3. To deal with a recruitment specialist.

All of these three methods would easily be helped via networking. So if you want a career move – get out there and network!

SUMMARY

We continued the discussion of networking in this chapter and looked first at who is in your current network. This includes all the people you know – at work or at home, past and present, those you contact by phone or by email, and those in online social networks. When listing these people you should note their jobs, interests, locations and so on and also consider how many people they know – this will show you the breadth of experience and contacts you have.

Next we looked to the future and who might come into your networks. Choosing new networking contacts can be done with a purpose such as developing your career or to raise your organisation's profile and this will influence your choices and actions.

An active approach to networking will ensure a more successful outcome and we looked at how you can prepare yourself, set objectives for your networking, approach people and then make use of your networks. Getting benefit from your networking efforts involves collating all the information you have collected and then following up with a letter or a note. After this it is essential to establish yourself as a useful contact and this can be done by finding a reason to contact people in your network on a regular basis. This could be sending them information that you know they will find useful, news about yourself or someone who your network contact also knows, or setting up a meeting with a specific purpose.

One purpose that you may have in networking is to find a mentor and we discussed the sort of person you may be looking for and how this could be done.

Finally, we discussed the importance of thanking people for any help – however small – that they may give you. And we saw that frequent and appropriate contact will lead to successful networking.

ACTION CHECKLIST

1. Decide upon your main purpose for networking – is it to gain information about your industry, to raise your organisation's profile or to raise your own profile?
2. Decide upon and set up a system for record keeping about your network.
3. Compile a list of all the people in your network.
4. Note anyone in your list who could help you with your main networking purpose.
5. Look at the list of people in your network and think of ways that you could make contact now with five of them – then do it.

ACTION CHECKLIST

12

The Companion Interview: Andy Green on Managing Yourself

The following interview with Andy Green was conducted by Ed Peppitt, author of *Six of the Best* (Hodder), when Andy was CEO of BT Global Services. After spending time with Shell and Deloitte Haskins & Sells he began a career with BT spanning over 22 years. In 2008 he moved to become CEO of business and technology service company, Logica. In his interview Andy clearly defined his personal take on managing yourself by breaking it down into five key topics and emphasising the importance of personal dynamism and motivation.

Ed Peppitt writes:

Of all the interviews I had prepared for, the subject of 'managing yourself' was easily the most personal. After all, it would be challenging to question someone about how people should manage themselves without getting to the heart of how the person I was interviewing manages himself. If I was to do this topic justice, I thought, I would need to establish what this person is like at home as well as at work. What are they like with people? How do they handle stress? How do they set their own agenda? How accessible are they to their colleagues and staff? What are their own goals and aspirations?

I needn't have worried. Andy Green, Chief Executive of BT Global, had also found time to prepare for our meeting before I arrived. He had thought about how he manages himself and had broken down what he wanted to say into five key topics: managing your time; managing yourself mentally; managing yourself physically; managing your image; and managing your growth. I was reminded of the assertion that if you need something done urgently, you should ask someone who is already busy. That statement was written with Andy Green in mind.

Dynamism

While preparing for my meeting, one of the documents I read was a paper published by the Chartered Management Institute. It said: 'Organisations and individuals need to be more dynamic if they are to succeed in today's global and competitive economy, but the energy levels required to be dynamic are heavily dependent on motivation.' I chose to kick off the interview by asking Andy if he agreed with this statement.

AG: I think it is an insightful statement if you mean 'dynamic' in the right way, and could be completely misleading otherwise. People say lots of things about what makes a good leader, and the biggest correlation is intelligence. But not everybody is intelligent, and some great leaders are not particularly bright. But they are all dynamic in the sense that they are questioning and challenging and they don't believe that the status quo will lead to success in the future.

If dynamic means the ability to recognise that you have to change and evolve, then I absolutely agree with that. I would say that regardless of the personal characteristics of leaders, I can't think of anybody whom I would class as a great leader who is not dynamic in that sense. But if it is suggesting that a leader has to be dynamic in the sense that they must be able to step on the stage and say 'rah-rah' to a sales force, I don't agree with that at all. I think there are many great leaders who have never done that.

So I would absolutely agree if we mean dynamic in this questioning sense, the search for a better way of doing things, an awareness of what is going on around you, a belief that the world is changing all the time and an acceptance that we have to change to be successful. In that sense I believe 100 per cent that dynamism lies behind all great leaders.

Given that definition, do you look around you at your peers and your colleagues and see a lack of dynamism, or plenty of dynamism?

I think that in any large organisation you are going to see more dynamic people rise to the top, although you'll find variations in that. I think it is very difficult to get good business results in the medium term without a dynamic view. I think there are a lot of companies out there who are quite complacent, and I have consistently said over the last few years that this is the most dangerous time to be complacent. The technology wave that we all talked about in the late 1990s is happening just a few years later, and if people aren't changing the way they are thinking about the world and globalisation, if they are not thinking about how technology is changing their business models and how they need to change – they will get left behind. You can see in every sector, that some people are really getting to grips with what is possible and others are falling behind.

It is very easy when you start a new job to change things. I think one of the challenges as you go through more and more business cycles is to rethink. When we have meetings I try to do them in different places, because anything you can do to keep the world looking different seems to me quite important.

So do you despair when you read about chief executives at BA who still print out their emails and pass their replies to their PAs?

Well, that is a different question I think. I recently heard a very good speech from the Chief Executive of a significant national body who stood up and said 'I don't have a computer'. Nevertheless, he still talked about the way they'd used database technology and deployed it to win a major international coup for the UK.

Managing your time

So Andy Green was endorsing the need for people and organisations to be dynamic, in the sense that they must recognise the constant need to question, change and evolve. I remembered reading that Andy had a passion and understanding of technology, and was a great believer that it will change people's lives for the better. So I asked Andy about how he used technology as part of managing himself.

On a personal level, I am completely embedded in technology. I am an active 'per the second' individual, but for most people that is not necessary. It is not necessary, not even good management at times, although I think personal management of time is very important, and technology can support that.

You mentioned that you are completely embedded in technology. Talk me through it. If you are sent an email, does something flash in your pocket?

Yes, absolutely. Technology-wise I use two things: my Blackberry, which I carry around the world, rather than a laptop; and my iPhone, which I carry around the world for all sorts of reasons, both business and pleasure. These days I even take the videos people want me to review on my iPhone to watch on the plane. There is a lot of video material; people will video a process, or the way a system works, and ask me to comment on it. Or I will look at a communication video that has been shot and I will check it to see whether I like what's been said. But generally the iPhone is a relaxation tool and to keep on top of my personal life.

So those two are there all the time. They are very active. Now in a big customer service organisation operating across the world like mine, where somebody is working 24 hours a day, the technology is good for increasing responsiveness at a time when our customers need us to be very responsive. That is excellent. But it is pretty bad for giving me thinking time. If I let it, it will stop me taking blocks of time to talk to people or think through things with people, or just think through things on my own. And I think the danger that I would recommend everybody watches out for, is that it could prevent you from having thinking time. You can't be a good leader unless you allow yourself to have enough thinking and planning time. I think it's crucial.

And how do you do that?

You just refuse to take the technology with you into meetings or similar types of situation. You have to cut yourself off, and make sure that you have people around you who can deal with urgent issues when you're not doing it.

Because you've got the technology, and because they know what sort of a man you are, do people expect instant responses to emails and texts?

Yes, often those who work closely with me in particular get very used to instant responses. That is good at one level. I operate on a global basis so I do a lot of travelling and there is a lot of time going into and out of airports when you can keep the business running with very low overhead costs to yourself. Filling dead time up is one of the things I like to do and technology really helps with that.

But time management is much more important in other ways. In a very senior role, there is a lot of management to do. You use a big chunk of your time taking part in the management team of your boss (in my case in the board), another in your own management team, and making sure that your people know what they are doing and that their performance is reviewed, and so on. And that's a lot of time. Then you will almost certainly spend a sizeable chunk of time on external things: It could relate to customer activity (in my case, it is heavily customer-oriented) but might also relate to shareholders or people – the set pieces or the communication activities that you do. I then leave a lot of time for what I call 'issues' ...

And is that what you referred to earlier as 'thinking time'?

No, thinking time would be a combination of issue time and the time I spend with my management team or with the board, because some of that is done collectively, and some of it is done on your own.

'Issue time' is, for example, when we are in the middle of considering an acquisition, and I would want to go and meet the management team; or we have a particular customer problem. I sometimes go right down into the detail if I think I can get my organisation to learn something by me doing it. I often encourage people to escalate what seems like a very small problem, if it's an illustration of a class of problem, because by giving a demonstration of how an issue can be resolved you can make a significant difference.

In your personal development, thinking about how you spend your time is a very important thing to do. How much is work? How much is home, or whatever else you do? How much is development and networking time? How much time are you going to choose to spend on each? How much time do you spend on management tasks such as customer and people issues? Do you leave yourself some time for what is urgent? Do you accept that some of your time has to be spent on tasks that vary from time to time? I find people get trapped into the way they run their time. I do too. I have to have people close to me who will force me to change the way I operate my time, otherwise I like to be available to everyone and talk to all sorts of people about many things. You have to force yourself to decide quite carefully how you use your time.

I am sure that no two days are the same, but do you devote time at the beginning of the day to plan how much time you are going to spend on each element during it?

No. I think most senior people live their lives in 15-minute blocks, with very, very little ability to exercise much change during the day without letting people down. One of the things I've discovered is that as you become more senior, at least 80 per cent of your meetings are more important for the person who is meeting you, than for you. But for you to help them and get full value you have to be respectful and give them equal importance. So we have to plan further in advance than each day. Normally I would plan two or three weeks in advance in detail. Some things are planned months and months in advance, like board meetings and things like that. Two or three weeks in advance in detail, and then as you get closer at the beginning of the week, or more likely the end of the previous week, you can assess the urgent issues that have arisen, and that's when you get disruption and you have to knock out meetings. But if you are knocking out things in the middle of the day, that's very disruptive on other people. I would always try to avoid that.

I think very senior people don't get a lot of blank spaces in their diaries. But maybe it's a personal choice because some people do it very well! I don't work alone particularly well. I tend to work better in groups.

Finding time for 'management by walking about' is also very important. I think if you have got a factory then that is pretty obvious. But walking about offices is kind of a weird thing to do! But getting clear input from people at all levels in your organisation, in an environment where they feel they can communicate with trust, is very important. And that's what I mean by 'walking about'.

There are lots of structured ways you can achieve this. I do things called '12 at 12s' where we just get 12 people around the table and we use what is called the 'Chatham House Rules': we can talk outside the meeting about what was said, but we can't say who said what. We just have 12 people around the table at 12 o'clock. Well actually it's often ten people at one o'clock, but the principle is the same! Whenever I am visiting a city, anywhere in the world, I try to do a small meeting with a group of our people of all levels.

Will there be any agenda?

No agenda. I just say, 'What do you want to talk about?' The point about that is that that gives me a set of inputs. I tell them that there will be no action points for me out of this. It just gives me information. Similarly, I make time to go on visits where we talk in detail about what work people are doing. But I think in most very big organisations you have to plan these things carefully. I also do open forums. They give you a different perspective than small groups because people mainly want to hear and understand and often people, depending on their culture, will not raise the more difficult issues. You are much more likely to hear difficult issues in the smaller groups.

While we use electronic communications intensively (blogs, podcasts, global webchats etc.), a part of my time is spent getting input that wouldn't come about unless I was there in person. For example, there is virtually nothing so valuable to a business as spending time with customers. One of the reasons I travel so much is that, in the end, it is almost impossible to be aware of what a Chinese customer really wants without going to see a Chinese customer in China. In any case, I think that there is a leadership responsibility around presence. We use electronic communication for calls and video conferencing, but there is something enormously motivating for a team, and interesting to the press, amongst other things, about you being present in a particular location. So there is a need to balance all of that.

But I can't over-emphasise the importance of thinking about what you are doing with your time. When we talk about personal growth, I think that one of the most important things to do whenever you get a new job is to really *think* about time. In my case, I am not disciplined enough to make changes without support. So I need to have a colleague who will work with me to make sure that I don't say yes when I should have said no.

Managing yourself mentally

Andy Green had been talking about managing time, and had stressed the importance of building thinking time into one's routine, particularly when one takes on a new position or role in an organisation. Yet his last comment had surprised me. He had said: 'In my case, I am not disciplined enough to make changes without support. So I need to have a colleague who will work with me to make sure that I don't say yes when I should have said no.' Andy was with BT for almost 22 years, and was Chief Executive of BT Global from 2001. What makes someone with that experience want or need a support network around him? It surely can't be a lack of confidence? What would it be? I had to ask him.

I would say, when we talk about managing yourself mentally, that I don't think there are any perfect leaders. Everybody has very significant weaknesses. Good leaders build teams around them who deal with their weaknesses. So they are prepared to say, 'Look, I am not very good at that', and then make sure that they have somebody on the team who can deal with those issues for them. I have to manage myself to change. There are people who say I am relaxed – one or two people might even say I'm lazy! – that is a misunderstanding I think, but it is very, very important for me to recognise that I need more organisational support around me than other people do.

That is what makes a difference to you?

If I am going to be effective I have to use my time correctly, so I need that support. I also need people around me who are strong deliverers of concepts. I am strategy-led in the way I operate. I think about the future and try to work out an intercept path which gives us an advantage, and then I can drive the organisation in that direction. So I work best with individuals who will take an idea from me, work it out and come back to me and say, 'This is what we are trying to do'. Then we might have another good debate, and finally they will go off and do it. Those sorts of people are people who work better with me than the more wavy-handed strategists; although I need a few of them to tell me I'm stupid when I'm going off in the wrong direction! With them, I can have a good row working out what the issues are.

It is crucial that you think about what you're strong at, and how you build a team of people who are capable of delivering, because if you believe you are going to do it yourself, you are nuts. I run a 30,000-strong organisation and if all the decisions come to me then we are going to move at a snail's pace. So in my world, I am trying to get hundreds of people scattered across the globe who, given a situation, will think as close to the way I would think about it as possible. They will take responsibility, they will take a decision, they will move on. And I am trying to get enough communication amongst us all so that they don't go off and do exactly the opposite of what I would want to do in that situation. It is about having a shared mental model.

So there has got to be empathy?

Absolutely – 'What are we all trying to do?' I think what gives you power in an organisation is the ability to build a culture that creates shared understanding and purpose. And that's another reason for being out and about, for spending time with people. It is a crucial issue I think.

Crises

When I met Andy Green for the first time, he had mentioned to me that he regarded managing oneself mentally as a vital skill for any aspiring manager or leader. I had already learned that part of that involved being mature enough to recognise your own shortfalls, and accept that you are not going to be able to do everything yourself. But what other skills make you mentally fitter to manage?

I have learned myself, and I would advise anyone keen to develop their career, to 'run towards the fire'. There's nothing like dealing with the biggest crisis you can find to learn about pace, organisational change and ambition. And let's face it, you are hardly likely to make a bad situation worse! It's a great learning experience. A crisis will demonstrate to you the people who you can rely on in the world and will also teach you the most valuable management skills. A lot of people walk away from crises. If you are ambitious, my advice is to get in there and help out. In tense situations, you develop true networks, people who you know you can work with over long distances and over a long period of time.

Is there a particular crisis that moulded your career?

My career was built on something called payphones. I was on the point of leaving BT because I had had enough after about 18 months. My boss then, Duncan Lewis, asked me if I would like to fix the payphones. I was supposed to be doing IT marketing, so I thought that was an interesting concept, and I was given about six weeks to fix a payphone system which had been broken for about 20 years!

It seemed like an impossible task. The payphones had been out of action for so long, mainly because customers didn't bother to report them. So even if we fixed them on the day they were reported, we would still miss the target that we had given the government. For years, we had been shouting at the engineers to move faster, but it didn't matter how fast they moved! So the first thing we did was to stop shouting at them, and they loved that.

We still needed a solution to the problem. We realised that we needed to check all the payphones, but how do you go about checking 100,000 public payphones? Eventually, the brainwave came and we found a merchandising company who stocked supermarket shelves. We gave each of their merchandisers a rota of payphones to check, and the problem was solved. Funnily enough, payphones went from losing £60 million to making a £90 million profit, simply because customers could put their money in!

I specialise in the idea of quick response. I honestly believe that a lot of people sit around and wait for long-term solutions to the problems. What do I mean by that? Well, take the issue of the payphones. It was quite clear that the root cause was that the payphones were supposed to self-report, and they didn't. So we could all have sat around and said, 'Well the problem is that the payphones don't self-report'. And we would have worked on that and done nothing else. And in three years' time we would have installed some new payphones, by which time our brand would have been in tatters.

Stress and the work/life balance

Stress is a part of our working lives in the twenty-first century. Few would argue that successful leaders seem either not to suffer from stress, or they have learned to manage it. Although many who fail to manage their stress effectively endure physical symptoms, the reality is that dealing with stress is largely a mental battle.

I was acutely aware that I was sitting on a sofa alongside one of the calmest people I have ever met. So does Andy Green understand what stress is all about? Does he suffer from it and, if so, how does he manage it?

One of the most important things about stress management is to accept the world as it is. I think most people's stress comes from wishing the world was something else. One of the things I think I am very good at is if, for example, I've got a great player who is on my side and they quit, or I have invested a long time in a contract or a piece of M&A [mergers & acquisitions] and it goes away, then I get over it. I might be grumpy for 30 minutes or need a glass of wine in the evening, but I am over it. The next day I am thinking about what's next, and I am not looking back.

I think that you reduce your stress level enormously by living in the real world as it is today and by keeping up with it.

The other thing that reduces stress is believing you are in control. Now you may say this is delusion, but I always say to my children, 'Try to do unto the world, not to be done unto'. This is not meant in an aggressive way at all, rather it is about a mental attitude. If you say, 'This is my problem, I have chosen to do this work, it is my job to employ everybody around me to get the right result', then you feel as though you are in control of the situation and you plan and think your way through it. The times I have seen people get most stressed (and I try to get my managers to understand this) is when you put people in a situation where they have no choice. For example, saying to someone, 'You have got to come in and work on Saturday come what may', and they think 'and next Saturday, and one after that' without giving them a sense of the future and giving them no choice in the matter you create stress.

One of the things about my story about payphones is that in situations like that I am painting a picture for everybody that says, 'However hard it may seem now, trust me, this is what is going to happen in the future', and then making that happen. Creating a culture with a sense of, 'You follow me, we will all do this together and however difficult it may feel right now, there is an answer at the end' – I think that reduces everybody's stress.

But it is also about how you can give people some control, and this is true about work/life balance as well. Work/life balance is not, in my mind, about the number of hours you spend in one place or in another place. What matters to people is, if you really need to be at the school gate at 4.30 p.m. on a given day, or every day then you can do that even if you work loads of hours in the evening. What stresses you is the inability to be able to be at the school gate on time – it is not about how many hours you are being asked to do, rather it's the inflexibility of those hours. So for different people at different times, what actually constitutes the stress point between the home and their work is very different. And you know, we don't talk about it. How many times does a manager sit down with the people they are responsible for and ask, 'What really matters to you at home? When I am arranging meetings and things like that, what should I watch out for you? How can I help you feel better?' It is often the smallest things. I personally don't think this is about work/life balance, it is about how we all understand each other's stress points and how we can avoid them.

And, from what I understand, about what matters to people?

What matters to *individuals*. Somehow that needs to be assessed in individual conversations and we need to be more respectful. For example, when you are sitting in a project team meeting and Fred has disappeared, we need to be respectful that that's Fred's point of pain. However, if he's always away then that's another issue altogether. But we do need to be respectful.

The other thing I believe about work/life balance is *being there*, mentally. I think the worst thing I can do is to turn up at home with my mind still full of work and not listen to a word of what's being said around me. I went through a period of quite significant rows at home with the family because I would walk in, not very early anyway, and I would not be completely with them.

So what changes have you made that have enabled you to arrive home and accept that you can switch off now?

Deliberately thinking it through and deciding that was what I was going to do. On occasions now, I will stay away when I don't actually need to be away from home, just because I am so hyped up with a load of stuff that I know if I go home it is just going to cause chaos. But when I am at home, I am actually doing the things that I am supposed to be doing at home and not doing things that I am supposed to be doing at work.

So let's just pursue that for a minute. You get home, you have opened a bottle of wine, you have switched off, and then your pocket vibrates because your Blackberry has received an email. What do you do?

My Blackberry doesn't vibrate ... although my phone does! If my phone vibrates then I will probably answer it because it could well be a personal call. So I will check who it is, and depending on what the situation is at home I might or might not take the call, but I would think about it very carefully. In terms of my Blackberry, I find it a good thing, especially when I am on holiday. Being able to receive emails stops me having lots and lots of phone calls because 20 minutes of emailing on the Blackberry at the end of an evening, or the end of a day when you are on holiday, can clear 90 per cent of things. You can decide for yourself whether there is anything that really needs to be done, because you are not having to keep phoning people back. If my daughter hadn't grassed me up, I think nobody would ever have known that I had a Blackberry, but she is too observant of these things!

But regarding work/life balance ... to be honest with you, the technology does matter and people talk about it a lot. One of the techniques I espoused at this year's World Economic Forum, when I presented to a workaholics seminar, was not to take your Blackberry battery charger on holiday. It is quite feasible to go two weeks on one battery on a Blackberry as long as you only turn it on for 20 minutes a day. I said that if you really, really can't do it, then I don't advise just cutting yourself off completely, because you then just end up making phone calls which are much more disruptive in my view. So these are just some little techniques you can try.

But that is just technology. The other aspect is the human aspect. The worst conversation I have probably ever had was with my now 13-year-old, who was six at the time. He said, 'Dad, your boss is so horrible, he makes you work so hard ...' and I sat down with the whole family and said, 'Look guys, we have all got to understand that dad works hard because he loves work. I go to work because it is great for us all, for our standard of living and all those things, but I am basically there, because I am happy when I'm at work, and when I come home I want to spend time being with you. But if I mix the two things up it doesn't work very well. I've got a big job which I love but you really can't blame my boss, because my boss never tells me what to do.' Nobody tells you what to do at senior levels, you are deciding these things for yourself. So my advice is, if you have got to work at the weekend, decide what time you are going to work, tell everybody that's the time you are working, and then don't work after it. Don't let it drift on throughout the weekend.

And have you stuck to that?

I stick to it mainly. You know, I had a very busy week last week, and I sat down in the garden working on paperwork for a lot of Sunday. It was all right because everybody was busy, and when they came up to me, I stopped. But it is not ideal. I would personally prefer to do less and less of that sort of thing. I try to avoid long periods of weekend working if I possibly can, because it is pretty busy the rest of the time.

I think one of the challenges of people discussing the work/life balance is that they see a balance as the same amount of each. They assume that if you have got too much of one then you haven't got enough of the other ...

I think it is about managing yourself mentally. I think you have to decide for yourself – it is quite selfish – what is right for you. I really think it is important that we respect each other on this sort of thing. What worries me mainly is setting an example. I think some senior people often set the worst example because they set up a pattern in people which says that the only way you can succeed is by working lots and lots of hours.

So what do you think about organisations that instil a long hours culture?

They worry me. On the other hand, it would be impossible for me personally to say that I am going to work nine-to-five because that's a better example for everybody. I would hate it, it would drive me absolutely nuts. Somehow, we have to find a way to communicate about these things amongst ourselves.

Just to recap on the stress side, what I have heard is that you must take responsibility, live with the present, forget the past. If something has happened, accept it and move on.

The final thing I would say about it, is that it is much easier to be less stressed if you have a relationship with your boss that has a good degree of trust in it. I argue creating that trust is my problem – I don't argue it is my boss's problem.

If you want a trusting relationship with your boss, then sitting there and waiting for your boss to create a trusting relationship with you is not what I would recommend. Personally, as part of wanting to be in control to reduce my stress levels, I have always taken it as my responsibility to manage my boss – to understand what is important to them, to work on that, to make their life as easy as possible, and to create a relationship where, if I am in a point of great uncertainty or things are very tough they will support me. I will stand in for any of my people at the drop of a hat and hope my boss will do the same for me. If it gets to the point where, for one reason or another, something can't be done – whether it is a personal thing or a work thing – they would turn up for a meeting for me. I will turn up at a meeting for my people, and I think that this helps with making people feel in control. I think this is a very big issue. It is a bit like the Hawthorne experiment that I always remember from my A levels, when you install something which allows people to stop the conveyor belt when they are working on a production line and they all produce much better work, feel much better, even though they don't ever pull the thing. I think there are deep psychological lessons in that for us all about being in control.

The other thing I would say about stress and senior management is that while some people would call me relaxed, I would say I am calm. The worse a situation gets, the more in crisis it becomes, the more I try to be a centre of purposeful calm. I do not want to be screaming and shouting and sending out random instructions. I don't want to be putting too much pressure on places where you can tell the pressure is already hot enough – there is no more they can reasonably do. So I am consistently trying, as things get tougher and tougher, to be more and more thoughtful, rational, calm and reassuring to people about what has to be done – often quite forceful and directive in moments of crisis, but not spreading pandemonium and stress, because I don't think that helps get you out of crisis.

What I am hearing is that one of the key ways to do that is to accept the crisis.

Absolutely.

And would you say that in some crises the people who are stressed are people who are effectively trying to fight the crisis?

I think that as a manager you have to accept that what you do makes a big difference, so you can easily stress your teams out. And you have a bit of a problem if you are in a very large organisation. I know that we are very results-driven, that I am a very results-driven person, and that creates enormous pressure down through the organisation – not because of screaming and shouting, but just because everybody knows that that is what the place is all about. If you get to a weak manager then that can very quickly create stress for those underneath that manager, because a weak manager at a time of crisis or poor results will very often create confusion. Bad things get done in your name every day when you run a very big group. There is no doubt about that. But I think we can all work at this to help each other on this strategy.

I also ask my people to look out for each other. One of the things I continually do is say, you don't have to be in a boss relationship to look out for people, you can look out for each other.

And you would endorse that both professionally and personally?

Yes, absolutely. I think it is often quite difficult to spot stress in personal situations, but my guess is that well over 50 per cent of situations where people are seriously stressed at work are not actually primarily related to the work. They may be related to some part of work, but they are almost certainly primarily to do with their personal life. So people get stressed, I think, rather than work makes them stressed. And they get stressed for lots of reasons. Life is tough for lots of people in lots of ways.

Perhaps that is really where the attention for dealing with work/life balance tension should be focused?

I think many people can help each other. One of the things about a good organisation is when peers look out for each other and help each other, particularly in an organisation like mine where lots of people work in very diverse ways in different places around the world. So people you work with directly may not even be in the same town or even in the same country, but you will always be in some sort of work group, and so that type of thinking is quite important.

Managing yourself physically

When Andy Green told me that he thought he managed stress quite well, he is obviously right. He then added, 'I also often have a lot of adrenalin', as if this was a very good thing. I was a little surprised. My memory from Biology class at school was that adrenalin was essential for our 'fight or flight' response – the example given always seemed to involve our ancestors running away from some large carnivorous animal. In a modern business context, I can appreciate that adrenalin is great for getting something done. However, my understanding is that having lots of adrenalin in our bodies, which we don't do something with, is not good for us at all. So I asked Andy how he deals with it, and how he gets rid of it at the end of the working day?

I don't. I like to have a lot of adrenalin.

But clearly by the time you get off a train or get out of the car at the end of the day you have got rid of it, haven't you?

There is that I suppose. I think I am able to move things from the front to the back of my mind quite well. You can work off adrenalin on the trampoline if you want as well, or whatever you do with the family. But I would say the point about adrenalin is that I like to be under pressure. So I like it when we have got difficult things to do and we have got a lot of people to convince, I love that sort of stuff. I thoroughly enjoy getting involved with anything which is enabling the team really to drive forward, or where I can make a very significant personal contribution. It is great. Going out on a pitch with a sales team is a great thing to do.

But is the opposite true of you? What are you like if you've got too much time before an event?

Yes, I am a good 'first take' person – on a video, a second take is not likely to be as good as the first. But I think people are very different in those sorts of ways.

So would you consciously put off doing something because the adrenalin, the pressure, isn't yet there?

No, I like to be organised. You need to be confident that all the information you need is going to be there. I couldn't present my way out of a paper bag at 25, I was basically shy. And of course when you go into a very senior job you are not just presenting, you are on show all the time. That was quite tricky. It took me quite a long time to get used to it.

I think everybody should try to understand what they are good at. For example, I have a very slow patch in the afternoon. I am capable of sleeping on planes, getting off planes, going straight to work, working flat out, getting on another plane, and I haven't a problem with that sort of stuff. I can manage my jet lag. But if I am in the UK under normal situations, around two o'clock is not a good time to have a one-to-one with me. I am likely to nod off in front of you. I just have a very low physical battery. Some people are great in the morning, some people are great in the evening. People have different physical cycles, and you need to know them. The biggest problem I find is when you have got a poor relationship with someone and you need to make it better, and you've got different cycles is finding the right time to try to rebuild the relationship.

One other reason why people don't get on well in relationships is because some people think very fast and some people think much slower, not because they are less good thinkers, they just like to think things through and mull them over. If people have different cycle speeds, they find it very difficult to create a partnership that really works.

Returning to the question of how you manage yourself physically: I like to keep fit, not very fit, but fit enough. I have back problems and other things which I need to manage.

So is there a gym here?

There is a gym here, but I don't use it. I did yoga and now Pilates, and I think it is important to understand your diet and what you drink or don't drink. Some people drink alcohol and feel fine, but you need to know when and how you can do various things, when should you eat, when should you not eat. Particularly if you are running an international business environment, if you don't know how to manage yourself into sleeping when you have to be asleep and not sleeping when you don't, it makes the whole job much more difficult. Now you don't have to do it like I do, by filling the whole day. There are people I know who get off a plane and they need two hours either to rest or exercise, depending on who they are, but if they set their agenda up properly they are fantastically effective. Other people you find are almost crumbling around you because they are trying to keep up and just can't. If you are going to be in a senior position, particularly a global one, managing yourself physically is something everybody needs to think about. If you need down-time – take it. You just have to find ways around it. Now you can't always, but if it's a real adrenalin situation, mostly you'll get through it anyway, most people do. But I think that you do need to understand physically what you need to do.

I used to work in north-west London, and if my MD was in trouble we always knew because he would go for a walk in the Chiltern Hills. He'd be back in two hours, but he would drive off to High Wycombe and go for a climb in the hills.

Absolutely. Personally I think that is underrated. What do I think are the things that most correlate with people getting to the top? A will and a desire to get there. There is a correlation in intelligence. We have talked about dynamism, this sort of questing sense – and the physical ability to do it.

And from what you're saying, the 'physical' isn't just exercise, it's diet, it's sleep …

Yes, it is all the things that work for you.

Managing your growth

Andy Green had mentioned to me before the interview just how important he thought the issue was of managing one's personal growth inside an organisation, and throughout one's career. As you take on more responsibility in an organisation, what should you do differently? From a personal perspective, I have witnessed a number of very good workers who are promoted to management positions, and who then fail. Why is this? Andy takes the issue very seriously.

The biggest mistake I see people make is that they go up a level in an organisation, or they get a more senior position, and they don't change what they do.

So what changes are necessary? What advice would you offer someone whose role and level of responsibility was growing inside an organisation?

If you consider the issue of managing growth, it brings a number of threads together. I think this is probably one of the most important things for individuals to think about.

One of the pieces of advice I always give to people is that if you are a manager who wishes to grow, or take on more responsibility, then you need to look at what your role comprises. It's very rare in today's information world for someone only to be doing management. You will also have your own set of tasks to perform. And I would say that whatever tasks you are responsible for, make sure you do them very well. That is priority number one.

Secondly, you need to develop yourself as a manager. Learn the skills of a manager. Learn how to make the people who are working for you effective.

Thirdly, try to help your boss do a great job. Help your boss, and they, in turn, will be thinking about the role you are performing in a much wider context.

And the final thing is this idea of what at Shell we used to call 'helicopter'. Are you somebody who is able to rise above what you are doing? Can you see the environment, the customers, the technology changes, the company, and say, 'Well, actually, we should be doing something different here'. What's significant is that you are not focusing solely or narrowly on your own personal objectives, you are thinking about how dynamically you can change what is going on around you and how you and your role fits in with everyone else's.

Shell called it 'helicopter'. It sounds similar to the NLP (Neuro-Linguistic Programming) technique of looking at a situation from a number of different positions or perspectives?

Absolutely. And I think it is really important, this ability to place what you are doing in context. It's one of those things that sets people apart. Some try to do it while forgetting the first three points. You tend only to get away with that when you're young, because business people are inclined to forgive a bit at the start of your career, and so they should.

But that leads to the next important point: Mistakes are excellent for learning. You can learn so much when you make a mistake. I have personally found that that is particularly true of mergers and acquisitions. Every time you go into a merger and acquisition transaction and decide not to do it, you still need to treat it as a success and a learning opportunity. It can be very hard for a team because they have usually spent a lot of time on it, and then you decide that you are not going to do it. There are lots of situations like this, and they create fantastic learning opportunities.

And how about recruitment? Does the sort of people you should recruit change as you grow in an organisation?

When people move into a new role, generally they continue to recruit the same sort of people they had in their last role. They don't say, 'I need somebody who is like I was two years ago, a different level of person'. Very often they find it quite difficult to recruit people at the right seniority because they have been promoted up through an organisation. Particularly somebody like me who stayed with one organisation a long time – people remember you and they may say, 'What's he doing up there?'

And therefore you have to put particular energy and effort into doing the right things. And that includes, as you get older, asking yourself what are the right external things for you to be doing – which conferences should you speak at, which dinners you should go to, all those types of things – as well as how you spend your time internally on what you do, how you project the position you are in.

It is really surprising how often that is at the heart of people who are doing really, really well, and then they suddenly stop. They have taken on a new set of responsibilities, they are still great people, they are doing their task very well, but underneath them they don't have the structure and they are not positioning themselves externally and inside the organisation in a manner which enables them genuinely to take on that role. Sometimes it is about doing it but not feeling quite comfortable with the people they are now peers with, and so mentally re-adjusting yourself to your position all the time as you go through your career is an extremely important part of what you need to do.

So you are newly promoted, and you have got new responsibilities, new levels of management. Two or three tips – where would you start?

I would start with my time. I would start with saying, 'Who are the most important people whom I have to work with to get done what I have got to do?' I would make a conscious effort to make sure that I was operating at the right level. Not because I am status-conscious – but because I am in a position to influence people at a certain level. That is part of what happens in life. Personally, I never lose my network of people at all levels in the organisation because they are tremendously useful. I always say to people when they stop working for me, you haven't really stopped working for me, I am just lending you away for a while.

Now if you are supposed to be running a sales team of 200 and you are still going and seeing the same customers, and the same people are still coming to the rugby with you or whatever else, you are doing the wrong thing. You are representing your company, you should have a new group of contacts and you should be entertaining different people. That is an obvious example, but it actually occurs very often. So I would emphasise that very strongly.

The second thing I would say is that the first time you come to change your team, watch yourself like a hawk. The crucial thing is to try to recruit somebody better than yourself. Now nobody likes this. I have done it always. I have always tried to recruit people who are better than me, if not in everything, then at least in some things. A good plan, if you want to be really successful, is to have great people wanting to work for you and doing fantastic work. I personally would like to be sitting at home as much as possible doing nothing, so I think if I can find great people to do the work then I don't have to worry about it, because I know the results are going to come through and they are going to do it with good values, and do it well. Hey, that's fantastic! But the number of people who think, 'Oh I'd better not, they might show me up' – people working for you don't show you up, not if you are a good manager.

How far into your career did it take you to learn that?

I was in my mid to late thirties before I became aware that this is a big issue. I think that is partly because I was doing lots of fixing things. I didn't tend to have very big teams, I was leading across the organisation rather than dealing with teams. I think it was just one of those growing-up things.

We talked earlier about the importance of networking and building your own network. Have you always been a good networker?

No, in fact I'm a bit of a loner. I'm still not a great networker. However, one of my great strengths is reading a room. So from a very early age I used to have to go and present to the board on all sorts of things, and I would work out what I thought the positions of the various directors were going to be.

What form would that take?

I would research the individuals. I am the same when I work with the sales force today. I would research them and understand what they are like, understand what sort of angle they might come from, and then after the third or fourth time presenting to them you would know them a bit.

I start with going in with as much information as possible, but then the crucial thing is to *listen*. It still stuns me how often I will come out of a meeting with one of my sales people and their reading of the meeting will be very different to mine. Even now. And I look at them and I think, how could you possibly have thought that? Listening to what is not said in a meeting is very important, and it is something that some people don't seem to be able to do. The thing that I feel sets aside really top-level negotiators and some top-level leaders from other people is that they can understand what is going on in the other person's head. We have all been to those meetings where somebody has turned up with you and they have gone off in the wrong direction and done completely the opposite of what you would have chosen to do. And it is remarkable how many meetings go like that. You can be quite well prepared, and still find that one side or the other has gone off on a tangent and you have to find a way to pull things back on track.

Specifically it is about understanding the context of everybody in the room, and about increasing the precision of your listening skills. Very thoughtful listening: what are they saying, why are they saying that and not something else, and what are they not saying? It is hugely important, particularly in an international environment because you have then got an awful lot of cultural aspects to consider.

I was going to ask you that because presumably, in an international meeting, is must be tempting to attribute periods of silence to just a difference in culture?

There are all sorts of issues around that. If you go to a translated Chinese or Japanese meeting you are in a completely different world, and there are all sorts of different things to worry about when you are in a global environment.

But the same rules apply?

The same rules apply, I think, in the sense that you should try to practise really listening to people. As somebody once said to me, listening without preparing to reply. I don't know about you, but because I am quite an active person, if somebody starts saying something to me, they will be half-way through the sentence and I'll be thinking of what am I going to say next. But if you can actually spend some time listening to people and try to understand what they are saying properly, and then think about your reply, it may be a bit slower than you might normally be, you might even put in a couple of fluffy phrases to get your act together, but it is worth practising.

My own experience is that there are an awful lot of business situations where people seem unable to bear silence.

It really is worth practising – 'Am I really hearing what these people are saying, do I really understand where they are coming from?' Because I think it is still an underrated skill, and I think too few people are very good at it. If you have got a personal situation which is not going well, then you absolutely have got to try to shake yourself out of thinking of the person when they walk into the room, and instead really listen to what they are saying. If you're thinking, 'Well Joe didn't deliver for me last week, and I heard he said something nasty about me in the corridor the week before ...', when Joe opens his mouth, whatever he says, you have got that big tail of baggage, and the result is that you get these very locked relationships which you can't unlock.

I talk to people a lot about the 'prisoner's dilemma'. Sometimes I have to instruct my team, when they are in some confrontational position with another company or another department that we are going to assume a good response when we hold out an olive branch. We are going to assume a good response and we are going to drop our guard, and even if they come back and we get a slap around the face, we are going to do it again. I might change my mind after a few slaps around the face! But I think an enormous problem in both business situations between organisations, and particularly between individuals, is to break out of deadlocked positions, the need to break negative relationship cycles. Trying to unlock situations which are not going well by deliberately saying, 'I will accept that part of what is happening here is that I am seeing Joe through these glasses which are just filled up with all this negative stuff and therefore we are never going to break out of this' is an important technique. So take that on board, go into a meeting, one-on-one, and just turn it around to be a positive by saying, 'I am going to keep an open mind, I am going to think positively about this person and situation'.

Very easy to say, and you have clearly managed to master it, but for someone who finds it difficult to disregard the baggage and forget it, what would you suggest?

I have not found it easy to do that. Although I do find it easy to leave the past behind in terms of what has happened in the world, actually leaving the past behind around people is much harder for me. So I carry the baggage around of what people have done to me or I have done to people. One of the things that this is about is guilt, because very often these blockages come most because you have been unfair to someone and you feel guilty about it. So sometimes it is not something the other person has done, it is something you've done, but nevertheless it sets up these blockages between people. So I find it quite easy to end up in locked positions – unlocking them has very high value.

But it doesn't necessarily come naturally?

It doesn't come naturally, so you have to sit down and decide that you are going to do it. Now I use coaches, not in the same way as most people talk about coaches, but if I feel that I need to spend some time developing my relationship with some peers or with some colleagues or customers, I will pick someone to sit down and talk through the problem with. So if it is a team issue, I will pick somebody from the HR department who is in that area and we will have a really clear conversation about what I am feeling.

I am a great believer that you are more likely to change and be thoughtful about what you are doing if you share it with someone. I am going to go away on a team-building thing in a couple of weeks time with my team, and one of the things I will do at the end of it is say, 'OK, this is the contract I've got with you guys as a result of today. I am going to try to make these changes. I am asking you to pick me up when I don't do it.'

Now some people find that very threatening in a way, but why if you have got enough confidence in yourself and you really want to improve? I find that you need a friendly colleague who will say, 'Didn't you say you were not going to do that to people, didn't you say you were going to make that clearer?' One of the things people say about me, because I think a lot and talk very fast, is that I am not always very clear. So a very simple technique is to have somebody who can say to you, 'I really didn't understand that Andy', and for it not to be an issue, or for either of us to feel threatened by it. But rather where people are able to say, 'Yes, that's in the contract, we all agreed. We all know Andy's a bit fuzzy around the edges because he thinks in different circles, so let's batter this until we all really understand it because we'll be better as a team once we have.'

So the tip here is, if you are trying to develop yourself, share it with someone who you are prepared to discuss it with.

And be brutally honest about it?

Yes, be really honest. I am a strategically led person, but we have a house rule among the strategy team in BT Global services: they are absolutely allowed to tell me that they think I am talking rubbish, because it's that challenge that creates a lot of value.

So when someone picks you up on something, does it annoy you, or do you welcome someone challenging you?

I am like any other person. Depending on the basis of the challenge, usually it is fine. However, there are some people I wouldn't dream of authorizing to do it. You need to think about who is going to be saying it to you!

Managing your image

Earlier in our discussion, Andy Green had recounted a piece of advice he had been given about why he wasn't always treated by his colleagues with the seniority that his position merited. I asked Andy to tell me more.

One of the best pieces of advice I ever got was when I walked into my then boss's office and asked him why people didn't treat me as the Strategy Director of a FTSE 30 company? And he said that if I want to be treated like one, then I should act like one. And it was very straightforward. I think it was one of the four pieces of advice that have stuck in my mind over the years, because often we don't take on the necessary attributes of our new roles very quickly.

This piece of advice prompted a wider discussion about the importance of 'image' – though Andy was quick to point out that he was referring to the word in the context of the way that managers or leaders present themselves.

I think that one of the things we really need to be careful about, and which we haven't talked about yet, is that I think you have to be true to yourself to be a good leader. I think people know when you are not genuine very quickly.

Are we talking about you personally here, or just anyone?

Anyone. When I was trying to learn how to do presentations, it was terrible. I was reading the books and I was going on the courses and trying to do it that way, and eventually I had someone from the theatre, a dramatist, who came and worked with me on it – and she said, this is never going to work. You have got to tell a story, and you have got to tell it from your own personal point of view. And as soon as I absorbed the idea that I displayed my own personality when on the stage or anywhere else, then it started to come together. I tell it as a story. I will often stop in the middle of something and say, 'When I was thinking about this, the key issue here was with this', and then suddenly you have got a completely different Andy standing on the stage than somebody who is just reading a slide. So we each have to be true to ourselves.

I also believe that it is very hard to be a really good leader if people don't believe you are committed to the enterprise, to the journey, to the company, whatever it is. In fact, I think it is difficult to get good followership if people think you are in it only for the money.

I see that. But Andy, there must have been times when there was a change or a process where you thought, I just don't believe in this – what do you do then?

That's very interesting. This is the question about whether you want to be a shop steward or a leader? There is an aspect to this question relating to values. If something happened in the company that really compromised my values, I would leave. I have no hesitation about that and I would think most people you talk to would agree with that. But I frequently find myself at the wrong end of a decision, something I think is wrong.

And you then have to carry that decision forward?

The question is, 'What do I then do about it?' When I was younger I used to go in and say 'Stupid bastards, blah blah blah'. And that's what I mean by shop stewards. The shop steward manager listens to all the things people are saying, and then when they are delivering the message further down the chain, they discuss whether it is a good thing or a bad thing within the little group for which they are responsible. And what happens there is that you end up with people being more stressed because, if you think about it, they are not doing what I said earlier: they are not living in today's world. A decision has been made, but they are saying, 'Now wouldn't it be better if that decision hadn't been made'. And the leaders are not helping their people change their world in line with that decision.

So what I say to leaders, and what I try to do myself, is to accept a decision, communicate it, work out what it means for us, and get on with our lives. That's it. We don't then think about whether it was the right or wrong decision. The world is always interesting and things unravel sometimes, but that is what you have committed to do. So one of the things I say to lots of people is, 'That's the policy'. And they might say, 'Well it's the wrong policy'. My reply is, 'OK, let's go and work out if it's the wrong policy, and if it's the wrong policy, we'll change it. And then we will tell everybody about the new policy. But until we have changed it, that's the policy'.

Another important question is how to help people who have an issue. Do you give them an answer or help them find an answer? I mentioned earlier the '12 at 12s'. I don't take any action points myself, but I will say to people, if I was faced with that problem I'd do these sorts of things, go talk to that person, do this, that and the other. The alternative approach is to say, 'Well look, we have given so-and-so the task of leading this, I think your job is to get alongside them and make your concerns known to them, but you know, if that is the direction we are going in, make sure it works for us as an organization'.

I think good leaders are continually trying to give their team a sense that they are in control, that they are living in the now, and therefore they are taking in decisions coming from the organization from all directions.

Not all of which they will agree with.

Not all of which they'll agree with, but I think there is a huge difference between living with things you don't agree with and not living to your values. For example, there are some things that worry me a lot, such as the security of our people in different parts of the world. I really don't think anybody can instruct me to do anything I don't want to do in that area and expect to keep me in the company.

For example, I operate in 170 countries. I am sure some of my agents somewhere are doing some things which I personally would not approve of – it would be very difficult to believe that that wasn't happening. So where's the edge? The edge for me is commitment to making sure that everybody understands what is expected. If you see anything, deal with it. It's about trying to make sure that your audits and other checks capture the things that they should, trying to live your values in the real world. You can't, as I said, in a 30,000-strong organization assume that everything will be done by the book every day, but you can send a clear signal that you expect things to be done by the book.

So my view is that you have to ask yourself, 'Are you living in the real world? Are you a force for what you consider the good?' And as long as you are confident that your presence in the organisation has a positive effect, then you should stand by. But there are times when your value set prompts you to say, 'I'm off, because I am not going to be associated with a company that does that'.

Are those times pretty clear-cut?

I think they are clear-cut in today's high disclosure environments. Particularly as a board director I think you know when your values are seriously compromised, and you absolutely need to deal with it. But that's different from expecting that every part of your organisation should reflect your value set. You know, I like working in telecommunications environments, I think it is generally a good thing in the world. I think IT and communications are a positive thing, so that sits quite well with me. But if you get to be in a very senior position, you can't guarantee that every part of your organisation is running according your value set, all the time. You can try to make that happen, but you won't always succeed. So I think that all you can do is decide for yourself whether you are prepared to be a leader, but if you do, then you do take responsibility if something goes wrong, and you will have to make decisions that aren't always comfortable.

I sense that the biggest tip you would give to someone who is growing in an organisation and progressing through an organisation is to be true to yourself in terms of recognising your values, is that right?

Not just recognising your values – I think you need to develop a style which is true to yourself. I think good leaders, great leaders, show their personality. They don't try to make themselves into a mannequin – there are lots of those around, but they are not the great leaders in my view. The great leaders are the ones who people feel they know. People have heard them speak, and they feel they know a bit about them.

Conclusions and recommendations

Andy Green is a straightforward, unshowy man. His biography doesn't run into several pages of public awards, memberships or committees. Instead, his achievements speak for themselves. He has earned his position by delivering remarkable bottom-line success for one of the world's best known companies over a 21-year period.

Part of his achievement can be attributed to his remarkable people skills, which I had witnessed first hand. Here was a man who had told me that he didn't like the questions I had prepared, and had provided me with an alternative question structure in their place. From anyone else, that might well have irritated and unnerved me. Not so with Andy Green. In fact, using Andy's structure provided a logical and sensible progression for our discussion, and I was grateful to him.

Andy's approach to managing yourself considers five key topics: managing your time; managing yourself mentally;

managing yourself physically; managing your image; and managing your growth. He has plenty to say on each, although he was quick to point out that everyone is different. Managing your time, for example, is about taking stock of where you are at, and building in opportunities for thought, for planning and for issues. Managing yourself mentally is about accepting the world as it is. Do that, he says, and you instantly have the tool you need to manage stress effectively. It's also about accepting your limitations and being mature enough to build an effective support network around you. Managing yourself physically is not necessarily about pumping iron every morning, it's about knowing what your body needs to perform, and then providing plenty of it. Managing your image has nothing whatever to do with playing a role. It's about being yourself, about taking responsibility and about making sure that your people know you, your strengths and your limitations. Finally, managing your growth is about all of these things, and especially about recognising that you have to change the way you work, the way you recruit and the way that you manage as you progress through your organisation.

Managing yourself checklist

If you are assessing how best to manage yourself as a leader, here are some issues to think about. You might want to find a few, valuable minutes to take a clean sheet of paper and jot down any ideas that the following list generates.

Dynamist

Do you question everything? Are you always looking for a better way of doing things? Do you accept that you have to change?

Managing time

How well do you think you manage time? What role, if any, does technology play in the way that you manage time? Do you allow yourself enough thinking time? Planning time? Issue time? Do you ever stop and think about how you spend your time? Would you say that your work life and home life are well balanced? Are you 'trapped' in the way that you manage your time? Do you manage by 'walking about'? Would introducing '12 at 12s' work for you?

Managing your mental state

What are your strengths and weaknesses? Who around you can support you in the areas of weakness you have identified? Could you reduce the stress in your role by 'accepting the world as it is'? Andy Green stays fresh by constantly changing his working environment – what could you do to 'keep the world looking different'? Would you say that you are in control? What really matters to you at work? What really matters to you at home? If you suffer from stress, how much of it do you bring into the office from home, and how much is work-related? Do you understand what causes your people's stress? When your working day is done, and you are at home, can you switch off? Are you 'being there'? Are you a workaholic? Could you leave your Blackberry charger at home for a fortnight?

Managing your physical side

Are you someone who is always pumped up with adrenalin? How do you use it effectively? Are you a 'first take' person? What is your best time of day, when you are most effective? What do you do to keep fit? Do you understand physically what you need to do? How is your diet? How well do you sleep?

Managing your growth

How have you changed as you have grown through your organisation or career? Are you still recruiting the same sort of people? What effect would recruiting someone better than you have? Have you stopped to consider what your role actually comprises? How does your role fit in with that of your colleagues? Have you paused to think about how you could help your boss do a good job? Are you good at 'moving on'? In a disagreement, are you good at leaving the 'baggage' behind? Do you use coaches, either formally or informally? Do you share issues with other people, or are you determined to work them through yourself? How do you feel if someone challenges you?

Managing your image

Are you true to yourself? Are you genuine, or do you play a role? If you didn't agree with a major issue within your organisation, what would you do?

National Occupational Standards

This book covers the NOS Management and Leadership standards – Facilitating Change. The following table will help you to locate these competencies in the book.

Competency	Unit no.	Chapter	Chapter title
Manage your own resources	A1	2	What personal resources do you need to do your job?
		3	How would setting objectives improve your performance?
		4	How can you fill any gaps in your current skills?
Manage your own resources and professional development	A2	5	What do you need to do to develop yourself professionally?

Competency	Unit no.	Chapter	Chapter title
		6	How can you make the best use of your time?
		7	How does your work role fit into your organisation?
		8	How can you obtain, and then use, useful feedback?
		9	What are your personal values and how do they affect your career?
Develop your personal networks	A3	10	Can networking help you in your work role?
		11	How can you develop your personal networks?

Further information and reading

Useful organisations and websites

Chartered Management Institute
Management House
Cottingham Road
Corby NN17 1TT
Tel 01536 204222
For information about all aspects of management and management
qualifications.

Management Standards Centre
3rd Floor, 2 Savoy Court
Strand
London WC2R 0EZ
Tel 0207 240 2826
www.management-standards.org/home

Department for Business Innovations and Skills
Main Office
1 Victoria St, London SW1H 0EY
Tel 0207 215 5000
www.bis.gov.uk
For information about all aspects of business.

Official UK Government website
www.direct.gov.uk
For a wide variety of information including employment and education.

Learndirect
www.learndirect-business.com
For advice about all sorts of business training and courses.

Chambers of Commerce
www.chamberonline.co.cuk
Local Chambers of Commerce are good sources of information on a variety of local and national business matters.

Business link
Tel 0845 600 9006
www.businesslink.gov.uk
Business Link is a government-funded network of local advice centres for business.

Mailing Preference Service
www.mpsonline.org.uk
Freepost 29
LON 20771
London W1E 0ZT
Tel 0845 703 4599
Registering with this service will reduce the amount of junk mail you receive.

Useful reading

Bird, Polly, *Teach Yourself Time Management* (Teach Yourself) 2008

Baguley, Phil, *Performance Management in a Week* (Hodder & Stoughton) 2002

Deeprose, Donna, *Smart Things to Know About Motivation* (Capstone) 2003

Locker, T. and O. Gregson, *Teach Yourself Managing Stress* (Teach Yourself) 2008

Pedler, M. *et al.*, *A Manager's Guide to Self Development* (McGraw-Hill), 2006

Peppit, Ed, *Six of the Best – lessons in life and leadership* (Hodder Arnold) 2007

Tracy, Brian, *Eat That Frog! 21 Great Ways to Stop Procrastinating and Get More Done in Less Time* (Hodder & Stoughton), 2004

And other titles in the Instant Manager Series

Index